A BUMPER CROP

HEALTH
RIGHT

A BUMPER CROP

Anne Williams

J. M. DENT & SONS LTD
London

First published 1988
© Anne Williams, 1988

This book is set in 11/12pt Linotron Goudy by Gee Graphics Ltd
Made in Great Britain by Butler & Tanner for
J.M. Dent & Sons Ltd
91 Clapham High Street, London SW4 7TA

British Library Cataloguing in Publication Data

Williams, Anne
        A bumper crop.——(Healthright).
        1. Food: Dishes using seasonal fruit –
        Recipes 2. Food: Dishes using seasonal
        vegetables – Recipes
        I. Title
        641.6'4

ISBN 0–460–02486–8

Contents

Contents

Autumn

Winter

All the Year Round

To my mother,
whose talent, hard work and love of gardening
filled our kitchen throughout the year

Introduction

Fridays and Saturdays are the busiest days at my small local street market. Every stall is operating, the road is jammed with vans stacked high with fruit and vegetables. The stallholders turn up at seven or eight in the morning and for the next ten hours just sell, sell, sell. By the end of the day the gutters are littered with cabbage leaves and discarded tomatoes, boxes which once held produce from Spain, Italy, France, Kent and East Anglia are stacked ten high by the rubbish skip. The butcher is auctioning off the last joints of lamb at rock-bottom prices. By nightfall the street is swept clean and quiet, while back home fridges bulge and saucepans simmer.

How lucky we are to live in a country where there is no shortage of fresh food. In fact we have one of the greatest choices of fresh fruit and vegetables in the Common Market. Every night lorries thunder into Covent Garden wholesale market from all over Europe. Our airports daily channel through carefully packed boxes of exotic fruit and vegetables. British market gardeners and growers are up before the crack of dawn to ferry their produce to the wholesalers and street markets in our towns and cities. Covent Garden turns over £300 million a year and Spitalfields about £100 million. Fruit and vegetables are cheaper than ever, in real terms, and the whole of Europe is overproducing. There is a constant glut.

The problem, more often, is what to do with all this bounty in the kitchen. How many times have you snapped up a pound of mushrooms at half price at the end of the day, only to have them rot at the bottom of the fridge for want of culinary inspiration? Or bought a whole lamb at special discount from the freezer centre, to find yourself left with plastic bags full of the less popular cuts like the breast? Perhaps you, like me, have had to cut your way out of the back door as the homegrown mint, triffid-like, takes over, or anxiously watched rows of never-ripening green tomatoes on every windowsill in the house.

The word glut is an ugly one, yet describes the situation in a nutshell. It conjures up instant images of piles of unexpectedly surplus food, of a race against time to freeze, preserve or cook mountains of strawberries, sacks of Jerusalem artichokes and baskets of blackberries. Apples might be one of your favourite snacks – but when the lawn is littered with windfalls, you may despair over what to do with them.

This book will, I hope, show you not only how to deal with extra quantities of perishable fruit and vegetables, but also how to enjoy them in a variety of new and healthy dishes. If you know enough ways to serve parsnips, leeks, Jerusalem artichokes and rhubarb without getting bored, what is the point, in winter, of forking out hard-earned money on expensive French beans, courgettes and peaches flown in from Guatemala, Kenya and other far-flung places? Tinned vegetables always contain added salt and often about two teaspoons of sugar as well – not to mention the loss of vitamin C, B vitamins and flavour. If you cook the produce in this book in season, the cost of your fruit and vegetable basket will be slashed and your diet much improved. Cheap British seasonal vegetables have been neglected for too long and many younger people have never learnt to cook them.

In *A Bumper Crop* I hope I have shown how serving fresh fruit and vegetables in season is not only far cheaper but produces much more enjoyable meals. It is not just that the texture and taste are superior, but that the various kinds of produce within each season go so well together – redcurrants and melons, pheasants and chestnuts, broad beans and asparagus. In this way, too, even town-dwellers can become more aware of the different times of the year, and of how best to anticipate and enjoy them.

How many of us have roasted chestnuts in the fire or seen scarlet clusters of redcurrants lying freshly picked in a basket? Gone on blackberrying expeditions, or lifted the big terracotta pot by the shed to gather spring's first tender rhubarb stalks? Known the delicious anticipation of cutting the first asparagus from the earth in the early summer sunshine, or the taste of tomatoes grown in real soil? (Yes, real soil – did you know that commercially grown hothouse tomatoes spend their short span suspended in liquid protein, being fed by a computer?) We may not all be lucky enough to have gardens to grow our own, but there is still enormous pleasure to be derived from making the most of each season's bumper crop.

I am no purist, unlike a restaurant I came across recently which refuses to serve any fruit other than British-grown on its dessert menu – it must get a bit dreary in winter. I love peaches, avocados and aubergines, lemons are a staple of my cooking and I am glad that one can buy mushrooms all the year round. I have included these in the book, particularly since they are often cheapest at a time when our own supplies are at a low ebb. More than anything else, however, my aim has been to inspire you to take full advantage of seasonal gluts, so that a bargain buy of mushrooms or strawberries doesn't lie rotting while you think of a new way to serve it.

Each season has its own section, which includes a type of meat or fish which is least expensive at that time of year. I have also given recipes for making jams, jellies and chutneys, the age-old ways of preserving food, as well as providing a guide to freezing fruit and vegetables. I tend not to freeze much cooked food, as the quality deteriorates after just a few weeks, but I find my freezer invaluable for storing large quantities of fruit and vegetables, particularly the summer harvests.

The recipes here will give you new ideas for dealing with a glut of French beans, a special offer on courgettes, or the perennial cry after Christmas, 'Not turkey *again*!' But I also hope they help you remember what eating is really all about – a necessity but also a pleasure, something to restore and revive and, in these days of modern living, a way of being creative and in touch with the simpler things of life.

Ingredients

Most of us are now more aware of the effect our diet has on our long-term health and are turning to ways of cutting down on foods high in saturated fat like cream, butter and full-fat milk, as well as reducing our sugar and salt intake. This book reflects that concern, while still realizing that food is for pleasure not penance, and that a sensible eye kept on our diet nevertheless gives room for the occasional treat.

The butter-margarine controversy continues, with both sides claiming the other is equally bad for you. Personally, I like to cook a lot of things in a little oil, either sunflower or olive, which are low in saturated fats, but I still use small amounts of butter rather than margarine from time to time, since in certain circumstances it gives a better taste.

Low-fat milk, either skimmed or semi-skimmed, can be used in all the recipes here, although bear in mind that children up to school age who are thin or who depend heavily on milk in their meals do need the full-fat variety. Whenever I include 'cream' cheese, I have used the lower-fat sort, marketed under the brand names Quark and Jockey. Fromage frais, made from fermented skimmed milk, is not widely available yet, but is catching on as a substitute in recipes requiring cream.

It horrifies me when I think how we once used to sprinkle sugar on everything, including fruits like grapefruit, melons and strawberries that already contain ample natural sweetness. My sweet tooth is now not nearly so demanding, but fruit like black- and redcurrants are too sour for most palates without some sweetening. Wherever possible I have used honey in those recipes, but occasionally honey is not suitable and raw sugar has been substituted – either muscovado or as a last resort unrefined granulated.

Incidentally, castor sugar is no more processed than granulated, merely ground up finer. You can make your own unrefined castor sugar where necessary by grinding unrefined granulated in a coffee grinder or liquidizer.

I have kept salt to a minimum – it is unnecessary, for example, automatically to put it in the water when cooking vegetables. Likewise my conversion to wholemeal flour has been gradual but steady. Mixed in proportions of three or four to one with plain white, it makes a good pastry, and many sauces can be thickened with it, but I find white flour is better suited to some dishes and have indicated this where appropriate (in these instances I have recommended the use of the unbleached variety).

In 1979 the Conservative government set up the National Advisory Committee on Nutrition Education (NACNE) to 'provide simple and accurate information on nutrition'. The first draft of its report caused an uproar in early 1981, since its recommendations, if implemented, would seriously undermine the interests of the big food manufacturers and attempts were made to prevent the NACNE Report from becoming public.

Here is not the place to go into the whole issue (Caroline Walker and Geoffrey Cannon's book *The Food Scandal* explains it all in fascinating detail) but briefly the main recommendations were that we British as a whole should cut our salt, sugar and saturated fat consumption by half and our alcohol by a third, and increase our fibre intake by half (in the form of grains and fresh fruit and vegetables). In other words we should be consuming far more fresh fruit and vegetables to stay healthy. That doesn't mean eating like a rabbit, but simply returning garden produce to its rightful place on the table – not squeezed in beside the roast beef, but served with style, imagination and enjoyment. This book will help you do just that.

Jams and Jellies

Homemade jam knocks the spots off the commercial variety, particularly the cheaper brands, both in taste and cost. If you are passing a pick-your-own farm in summer, or are lucky enough to grow your own soft fruits, jams and jellies are delicious ways to enjoy the fruit well after the season has ended. It is a way of spreading your surplus throughout the year. That said, it should not be denied that jams contain a good deal of sugar (see below under ingredients) which is necessary to prevent them from going bad, so for health reasons it is not advisable to eat jam every day (or not unless that is almost the only added sugar you eat). A couple of times a week, as a treat with crusty wholemeal bread at the weekend, or a small spoonful of jelly with some cold meat or chicken, isn't cause for alarm, however, particularly if you have cut down on sugar elsewhere in your diet.

Science

Many people are nervous about making their own jam, yet although it is a skill which is becoming rarer these days, there is no need for it to be shrouded in mystique. As in all cooking, there are scientific reasons why things work and there are steps to take to avoid failure. I always say to people who claim they can't cook that they should be more confident; anyone who can read a recipe book can cook. However, there are certain rules you must follow, particularly in the preserving of food, or you won't achieve what you set out to create.

Pectin This is a setting agent in the cell walls of the fruit which, when boiled, is released into the liquid juices and dissolves. Different fruit contain varying amounts of pectin, which is the reason why some jams are much easier to set than others.

Fruit high in pectin	Fruit with medium pectin content	Fruit low in pectin
apples	raspberries	blackberries
redcurrants	apricots	strawberries
blackcurrants	plums	rhubarb
gooseberries		cherries
damsons		
quinces		

Fruit with a low pectin content needs to be mixed with either the pulp or the juice of a fruit high in it, which is why you find familiar combinations like blackberry and apple. Those with a medium content usually just need a little extra acid. When it is overripe, fruit loses some of its pectin content, so only pick firm, dry berries or currants.

Acid   This is needed to draw out the pectin in order to set the jam. It also improves the flavour and colour and prevents the jam from crystallizing. All fruits contain a certain amount of acid, but a tablespoon of lemon juice is an easy way of adding extra.

Sugar   However long the controversy rages over the effect of sugar on our health, there is no getting away from the fact that for domestic jam-making no really satisfactory alternative has been found. Sugar is essential for the preservation of the jam or jelly, as well as for helping it to set. If you cut down on the amount too much all that happens is that the jam will go bad. Sugar-free 'jams' currently on the market must be stored in the fridge once opened, and those made at home must often be refrigerated even before opening.

   The quantities given here are the recommended minimum for successful traditional jam- and jelly-making. Either granulated or preserving sugar can be used, and there is now a less refined granulated sugar on the market which is suitable. The advantage of preserving sugar is that it is less likely to crystallize and produces less scum, but it is not available in unrefined or raw form and it is not essential to use it. It is a good idea to warm the sugar first, in a pan in the oven or over a gentle heat, as this helps it dissolve more quickly.

Equipment

Pan   Any large saucepan, preferably of stainless steel, can be used, but make sure it has a heavy bottom or you may find the sugar in the jam will burn and ruin the whole batch.

Sugar thermometer   This is very useful for telling you when the jam or jelly has reached setting point. You can sometimes find them at jumble sales, if you don't want to buy a new one. The other method of testing for setting involves spooning a little of the jam on to a plate and trying out its consistency, but less confident cooks may prefer to trust science and use a thermometer.

Jars Any jar will do, so long as the glass is not too fragile or it may crack on contact with the very hot jam. Save ones previously containing coffee and so on. The best sizes are those of 1 lb (450 g), which is what most bought marmalades, honeys, etc come in, and the small ones in which horseradish and mustards are sold, which are useful for storing your homemade jelly. All jars should be absolutely clean before you fill them, as any bacteria will only encourage the contents to go mouldy.

Covers You need a good supply of waxed circles which lie on top of the jam or jelly, plus some transparent paper covers and elastic bands to fasten them. These can be bought in various sizes.

Labels Do make sure you label your jams and jellies, both with the fruit and the date made. Use a pen that won't smudge if you wipe the jar with a damp cloth to remove any stickiness.

Jelly-bag This is a cloth bag with a wide brim which you suspend full of cooked fruit from a hook. Overnight the juice drips through, and is then mixed with sugar for setting. A large piece of muslin can be used, if you tie the four corners round an upturned chair's legs.

To Make Jam

1. Remove any stalks from the fruit and if necessary wash briefly. Simmer the fruit in the pan long enough to break down the cell walls and let the pectin run out into the juices. Soft fruit like strawberries do not need any water, but it is advisable to add a little to other sorts in order to prevent them from burning.
2. Add the sugar and stir well over a gentle heat until it has dissolved completely. Then bring rapidly to the boil and, stirring occasionally, boil fast until setting point is reached. This will take between 5 and 20 minutes depending on the fruit.
3. To test for setting point, either use a thermometer to see if the jam has reached 220°F/110°C or try the plate method. With a teaspoon put a little jam on the side of a cold plate (best straight from the fridge), leave it for a second or two and then draw your finger through it. If it remains in two separate halves, it is ready.

   Setting point can be reached and passed quite quickly, so don't wander off for 5 minutes if your first test indicates the jam needs more time. Keep testing, for if overcooked it won't set.
4. Skim off any scum with a slotted spoon and pour into clean jars, right up to the brim. Cover the surface with a waxed circle, wipe any spillage off the outside of the jar, and fasten a transparent cover over the top with an elastic band. Label and store.

To Make Jelly

1. Since in this case the fruit is strained and only the juice used, there is no need to remove any stalks from the fruit, but wash it briefly if necessary before putting in a large pan. Simmer gently for 30-60 minutes or more until really soft, to allow the maximum amount of pectin to be released. Harder fruit like currants should be just covered with water, soft ones like blackberries need very little water added.

2. Put the fruit into the jelly-bag and leave suspended over a large bowl for 6-12 hours. Don't try and hurry it along be pressing the fruit to squeeze out more juice, this will only make the jelly cloudy. The pulp of fruit such as black- and redcurrants, which are very rich in pectin, can be mixed with about half the original quantity of water, reboiled and strained for a second time.

3. Pour the juice into a measuring jug before transferring it to a saucepan. Add 1 lb (450 g) of sugar to every pint (550 ml) juice. Those very high in pectin may require less sugar. (In the recipes here I have not generally specified the amount of sugar in the list of ingredients, since the final volume of liquid can vary so much according to the ripeness of the fruit and so on.) Heat gently, stirring, until the sugar has dissolved and then boil rapidly until setting point (220°F/110°C) is reached. If you don't have a thermometer, put a teaspoon of jelly on the edge of a small plate you have chilled in the fridge, leave it a second and then draw your finger through. If it remains in two halves, it will set when bottled.

4. Remove any scum and pour into clean jars before covering while still hot. Label and store after the jelly has set.

Storage

Jams and jellies should be stored in a cool dry place, preferably in the dark. Most kitchens, unless you are lucky enough to have a larder, are too warm and humid. A good idea is to use the garage or an outside shed, or even a cupboard in a spare bedroom where the heating is rarely on. In damp conditions a mould may develop on the surface. However, this doesn't mean the entire contents are inedible or that the jam is actually bad – just scrape off the mould before using.

Pickles and Chutneys

Pickling has been used in various forms for thousands of years as a method of preserving food. The term brings to mind vegetables stored in spiced vinegar, like pickled onions or red cabbage, but it also includes chutneys (what the Americans call relishes). Pickling surpluses of food is a cheap way not only of storing them for future eating, but of adding a completely new set of tastes to your storecupboard.

There are many different ways of preparing pickles, so each recipe in this book for a pickle or chutney goes into full detail on the method to follow. Here I give some tips to make sure yours are not only delicious and attractive, but keep well too.

Equipment

Never use a copper or brass pan to prepare your pickles and chutneys, as the acid in the vinegar will corrode it. Also be very wary of earthenware pots and dishes, which may have a lead-glaze which is extremely dangerous when broken down by the acid. (Modern earthenware is not usually lead-glazed, but check first.) Stainless steel or enamel is best. Once prepared, pickles should be stored in glass jars.

Vinegar

Originally pickles were preserved in verjus or verjuice, which was a kind of vinegar made from fermented unripe grapes left at the end of harvesting. This gave a mild taste and continued to be used right through the boom age of pickling – the Tudor and Stuart era – when it was the major method of food preservation. As trade with the East grew, more fruits and spices appeared in the kitchen and soon found their way into new dishes like more exotic chutneys. In the nineteenth century wine vinegar was superseded by malt vinegar for mass production of pickles. Adulteration of the vinegar used in these pickles had horrific consequences (some contained sulphuric acid !) and meant those who could afford it stuck to their own homemade wine vinegar.

White wine vinegar is better for those pickles with a more delicate flavour such as mushrooms, while malt vinegar is suitable for onions, red cabbage and so on. For a more attractive appearance you can use distilled malt vinegar, which has the same taste and keeping qualities but, being clear, brings out the colour of the vegetables better.

Storage

It is very important that pickles and chutneys are kept in completely airtight containers until you open them to eat. Over the years I have tried many different types of jars, and have found that money always wins in the end. The best are the heatproof, wide-necked Kilner jars with orange rubber seals held in place by a ferocious-looking wire lever. Although quite expensive, you can use them year after year, needing only to replace the rubber seals each season. Second to these are the screw-top Kilner jars, but I have found that the metal lids rust after a while.

The alternative is to use jars saved from bought marmalade and so on. This is fine if you're watching the pennies, but make sure you choose ones with a good thread on the screw – the plastic-lidded instant coffee jars aren't reliably airtight. It is better to use several smaller jars than one or two large ones, or once opened the contents may spoil before you have reached the bottom. (In fact it is always worth keeping opened jars in the fridge, to inhibit the growth of bacteria.)

Store all pickles and chutneys (as with jams and jellies) in cool dry dark conditions – an outside shed or garage is ideal. Humidity and damp will encourage the growth of mould and sunlight will eventually bleach the vegetables.

Freezing

The development of the domestic freezer can be seen as one of the milestones in culinary history. For the first time it became possible to store fruit and vegetables simply and cheaply, barely altering their flavour or texture. A family with a fair-sized kitchen garden can, with the help of a freezer, be virtually self-sufficient in vegetables and go a long way towards it with summer fruit.

A freezer is also useful for storing leftovers, to be eaten fairly quickly, as well as ice-cream, meat and fish. But its main selling point, I feel, is that it enables you to make the most of surpluses of seasonal produce. Having worked your way through every recipe imaginable to enjoy the crop at its freshest, you can freeze the rest to bring out later in the year. By taking advantage of cheap offers on whole lambs, for example, you can save yourself pounds over what you would spend if having to shop daily at non-discount prices.

There are plenty of books around on choosing, organizing and stocking a freezer. Here are just a few tips on how to prepare and store food for freezing.

Equipment and Packaging

A good supply of **rigid plastic containers** with clip-on lids is invaluable. These can be used again and again for purées, ice-creams, sorbets and soups. Square or rectangular shapes take up much less room than round ones since they stack better, so a good trick is to line a rigid container with a plastic freezer bag, fill with your soup or purée, freeze, and then remove the bag from the box leaving it free for future use.

Strong plastic freezer bags are essential, especially for storing fruit and vegetables, as ordinary ones are too thin to give adequate protection. An excellent mail order supplier is Lakeland Plastics, Alexandra Buildings, Windermere, Cumbria LA23 1BQ, who seem to be much cheaper than anywhere else and supply everything I mention below for the home freezer.

Twist-ties, labels and a waterproof pen will be needed. It is very important to label all food with the date you froze it, what it is and how much it weighs (or how many people it serves). Starting a log-book of what you have in the freezer is a good idea, if you are organized enough to keep it up to date.

Aluminium foil should be the heavy-duty kind, or it will tear too easily and give the contents freezer burn, which ruins the texture and doesn't do a lot for the flavour. It is useful for wrapping meat, poultry and fish.

Clingfilm is really too thin to give adequate protection in a freezer, although it's fine for wrapping a few parsley stalks in to save for stock-making. If you want to use clingfilm, you should buy the non-PVC variety, if it is going to come into contact with any food containing fat, and always overwrap it in silver foil. (Ordinary clingfilm is fine for covering the tops of bowls, etc.)

A plastic wide-mouthed funnel is handy for transferring beans and currants as well as liquids into bags, to prevent them from spilling all over the floor. It costs next to nothing.

You need a **chip basket** (clean) or other inner wire basket for blanching vegetables. By lifting it out you can use the same water for the next batch, instead of draining it away, thereby saving on time (and fuel).

Preparation

All food should be frozen when it is cold and absolutely fresh. Six months in the freezer is not going to improve the quality of something that was already past its best. After blanching or cooking, do not keep the food hanging around the kitchen, cool it as quickly as possible, pack, label and wrap. If your machine has a fast freeze button, this speeds up the process.

Blanching is really another word for scalding, that is immersing in boiling water for a very short time. You should blanch all vegetables before freezing (see table on page 13). The enzymes they contain, which over time would break down their colour, texture and flavour, are thereby destroyed. It is not dangerous to omit this stage, but unblanched vegetables have a much shorter freezer life – three months as opposed to about twelve.

Blanch small batches at a time. Bring a large pan of water to the boil, immerse the prepared vegetables, preferably in some kind of a basket, return rapidly to the boil and time them from this moment. Then remove them and run under a cold tap or immerse in a sinkful of cold water. When cold, drain, pack, label and freeze.

Many fruit and vegetables are easier to deal with and cook afterwards if you **open-freeze** them. Simply spread them on a tray (after blanching in the case of vegetables), pop in the freezer until frozen, then transfer to a plastic bag before labelling and storing. This means they will pour easily out of the bag, instead of sitting in their cooking water in a frozen lump, so the outsides are overcooked by the time the core has melted. All commercial peas, beans and so on are frozen this way and you will find it a good way to deal with a range of home-grown fruit and vegetables (see table).

Storing

Once cold, transfer the food immediately to containers or bags. It is air which spoils food while it is in the freezer, so exclude as much as possible from plastic bags and, if using rigid containers, leave only ½ inch (1.5 cm) or so at the top for normal expansion. Freeze everything in sensible portions for your household – if there are just two of you, there's not much point packing vegetables in 3 lb (1.35 kg) bags. Label clearly. You may like to use different coloured labels for easy identification of fruit, vegetables, meat, fish, pastry, etc. Likewise it is a good idea to separate types of food in the freezer – one basket or shelf for fruit, another for vegetables and so on. If you have a chest freezer, put the individual bags into a strong plastic dustbin bag, to save you from rummaging around at the bottom for a pound of beans.

Vegetables

Preparation and packing	Blanching time (minutes)	Freezer life (months)
Asparagus Wash, trim into even lengths. Add 1 tbsp lemon juice to blanching water. Freeze in layers in rigid containers, separated by non-stick paper.	2 (thin stems) 4 (thick stems)	9

Preparation and packing	Blanching time (minutes)	Freezer life (months)
Aubergine Slice thickly or dice. Add 1 tbsp lemon juice to blanching water. Dry, open-freeze then transfer to polythene bags.	4	12
Avocado Peel, purée with 1 tbsp lemon juice per avocado. Freeze in small rigid containers. For use in sauces and soups.	—	2
Beans, broad Shell, blanch, dry, open-freeze, then transfer to polythene bags.	2	12
Beans, French Wash, trim, cut in half if you like. Blanch, open-freeze, then transfer to polythene bags.	2	12
Brussels sprouts Wash, trim, grade into sizes. Blanch, drain well, open-freeze then transfer to polythene bags.	3 (small) 4 (medium)	12
Cauliflower Remove outer leaves, split into florets about 2 inches (5 cm) diameter. Blanch with 1 tbsp lemon juice, drain well, open- freeze then transfer to polythene bags.	3	6
Celery Trim, wash stalks well, cut into 2 inch (5 cm) pieces. Blanch, drain well, open-freeze then transfer to polythene bags. Not suitable for salads after freezing.	3	6
Courgette Wipe, trim, slice thickly. Blanch, dry and open-freeze; or sauté in butter 1 minute. Best in soups and casseroles, can go rather soggy.	1	6

Preparation and packing	Blanching time (minutes)	Freezer life (months)
Cucumber Unsuitable for freezing.	—	—
Jerusalem artichoke Unsuitable for freezing except in form of cooked soup or purée.	—	3
Leek Trim ruthlessly and wash well. Leave small ones whole, blanch, dry and freeze in polythene bags. Slice larger ones, blanch, dry, freeze in small quantities in polythene bags.	3-4 (whole) 2 (sliced)	6
Mint Wash, dry, strip leaves off the stalks. Freeze leaves in small bunches in polythene bags.	—	6
Mushroom Small button: wipe, open-freeze, then transfer to polythene bags.	—	1
Large: wipe, slice, sauté in butter 1 minute. Pack into small rigid containers with cooking liquid.	—	3
Parsnip Trim, peel, cut into batons or dice. Blanch with 1 tbsp lemon juice. Open-freeze, then transfer to polythene bags.	2	12
Spinach Easiest to freeze ready cooked. Strip off stalks, wash really well, cook 3-5 minutes in pan with no extra water. Press dry, freeze in small quantities in polythene bags.	—	12

Preparation and packing	Blanching time (minutes)	Freezer life (months)
Sweetcorn Trim and strip off husks and silky threads. Blanch, and either freeze whole, or strip off kernels and open-freeze, then transfer to polythene bags.	4 (small) 6 (medium) 8 (large)	12
Sweet pepper Wash, cut out stems and remove seeds. Halve, slice or cut into rings. Blanch, drain, open-freeze, then transfer to polythene bags.	3 (halves) 2 (slices and rings)	12
Tomato Not suitable for freezing whole. Chop, cook gently 10-15 minutes with a little seasoning and herbs. Then sieve or purée and freeze in rigid containers; or reduce and freeze in ice-cube trays, before transferring to polythene bags. Use in soups, stews, etc.	—	12

Fruit

Preparation and packing	Freezer life (months)
Apple Peel, core, slice, drop into cold water with squeeze lemon juice as you prepare each apple. Drain, blanch 2 minutes, drain, dry. Open-freeze then transfer to polythene bags. Use from frozen.	8
Or: peel, core, chop and cook to purée with very little water and 1 tbsp lemon juice. Pack into rigid containers in small quantities and freeze. Use from frozen or thaw 3 hours at room temperature.	6
Blackberry Only wash if necessary, pat dry. Open-freeze, then transfer to polythene bags or rigid containers.	12

Preparation and packing	Freezer life (months)
Overripe fruit can be cooked and puréed, then packed in rigid containers.	12
Thaw overnight in fridge or cook from frozen.	12
Blackcurrant Wash, remove stems and, if you like, the small end stem. Pat dry. Open-freeze, then transfer to polythene bags or rigid containers.	12
Thaw overnight in fridge, 3 hours at room temperature or cook from frozen.	
Lemon Halve and squeeze juice. Pour into ice-cube trays, freeze, then transfer cubes to polythene bag.	12
Thaw at room temperature or use from frozen.	
Peach and nectarine Prepare syrup: 8 oz (225 g) sugar to 1 pint (550 ml) water. Dissolve sugar, bring to boil, cool. Add 1 tbsp lemon juice to each pint syrup. Skin peaches, halve or slice, pack in rigid containers, pour over syrup, freeze.	8
Thaw 3-4 hours at room temperature.	
Raspberry Remove any stalks, open-freeze, transfer to rigid containers.	12
Thaw overnight in fridge.	
Redcurrant Strip off stalks, wash, dry, open-freeze. Transfer to polythene bags or rigid containers.	12
Thaw overnight in fridge, 3 hours at room temperature or cook from frozen.	
Rhubarb Wash, trim and cut into 2 inch (5 cm) pieces. Blanch 1 minute, drain. Then dry and open-freeze before transferring to polythene bags; or pack in cold syrup (8 oz/225 g sugar to 1 pint/550 ml water) in rigid containers.	12
Thaw 3 hours at room temperature or cook from frozen.	
Strawberry Best frozen as a purée, as whole ones are mushy after freezing. Liquidize or sieve, pour into rigid containers. Use for sauces, ice-creams, mousses.	12
Thaw 3 hours at room temperature.	

Other

Preparation and packing	Freezer life (months)
Chestnut Peel and remove inner brown skin (see page 120), freeze in polythene bags.	6
Or: peel and remove inner brown skin, cook in stock 35-40 minutes, drain, purée in food processor or sieve. Pack into rigid containers and freeze. Thaw overnight in fridge.	6
Lamb Wrap joints in thick polythene bags, excluding as much air as possible. Wrap and open-freeze chops before storing together in larger bags. Thaw in fridge allowing 5 hours or more per lb (450 g). Chops can be cooked from frozen but it is more difficult to get the timing right (i.e. pink in the middle).	6-8
Pheasant Pack in polythene bag, excluding maximum amount of air, after hanging, plucking and drawing. Thaw in fridge allowing 5 hours to the lb (450 g).	6
Salmon Freeze as fresh as possible. Scale, gut, wash, dry. Leave whole or cut into 2-3 pieces, or into steaks. Wrap in thick polythene and seal well. Thaw whole fish or pieces in wrapping, in fridge. (Whole salmon takes up to 24 hours.) Steaks – thaw in fridge 3 hours.	6 (whole) 4 (cuts and steaks)
Turkey Wrap in heavy polythene, excluding as much air as you can. Thaw completely in fridge. Small birds take 2 days, large ones 3-4.	6 (whole)
Cooked turkey can be packed closely in rigid containers for freezing. Thaw 3-4 hours in fridge, in container.	1-2 (cooked)

Note

A number of processes and cooking terms which
recur throughout the following recipes are
described and explained in full at the end of the book.

EARLY SUMMER

Asparagus

Cultivated asparagus, which is related to the lily family, has been grown in Europe for over two thousand years, although it was only introduced to this country a few hundred years ago. The edible parts are the young shoots, or spears, that come up every spring. Since asparagus takes up a lot of space and requires labour-intensive cultivation, the fat bundles that appear in our shops in early summer never hit rock-bottom prices.

Those lucky enough to have sufficient space in their gardens to tie up for several years in an asparagus bed, and the patience to wait two seasons before harvesting a single spear, are amply rewarded by a daily crop throughout the short season. The rest of us must pay through the nose for it, which means the more crafty ways you can find to make a little go a long way, the more you can enjoy it. I don't think personally that the imported white asparagus popular in Belgium and Germany is really worth buying, particularly out of season, for nothing compares with the flavour of the green-purple English variety.

Home-grown asparagus is in season for only about six weeks, from late May to the end of June. During those weeks asparagus lovers will be enjoying the crop to its full, and those growing their own will have daily harvests. It can become, even for the biggest fans, a little monotonous to eat it day after day just plainly boiled, dipped in butter or vinaigrette. I have therefore given a selection of recipes which will vary your diet of this delicious vegetable. For those who must buy it in shops, you will find here some new ways to cook it which stretch your small and expensive bundle into a whole meal.

Do not store asparagus for too long before cooking, a couple of days at most. If the stems are limp it is past its best. Tie the stems into bundles and cook them standing upright for 12-15 minutes or longer, depending on size. The bases rest in the simmering, slightly salted water and the tips cook in the steam that is given off.

If you are serving asparagus on ordinary plates, put your fork, prongs pointing down, under the plate on one side. This will tip it gently and ensure the sauce remains all at the side, rather than running all over the plate, the stalks and your fingers.

See also Broad Bean and Asparagus Salad.

Asparagus with Orange Hollandaise

If you like eating asparagus plain, dipped in butter and seasoned with a little black pepper or salt, a delicious variation is to serve it with a warm hollandaise sauce, which you can finish off while the asparagus is cooking. Or try this slightly more unusual alternative to the classic hollandaise.

Serves 4

2 lb (900 g) asparagus
3 tbsp tarragon or wine vinegar
1 slice lemon
small bayleaf
few black peppercorns

2 egg yolks (size 1 or 2 eggs)
4 oz (110 g) butter
seasoning
2 tbsp orange juice
2 tbsp grated orange rind

Put the vinegar, lemon, bayleaf and peppercorns into a small saucepan and boil until the liquid is reduced to about a tablespoon. Strain, pour into a heatproof bowl that will sit over a saucepan and cool slightly.

Wash the asparagus and cut off the thick ends. If the stems are quite large, shave the ends to get rid of any woody outside stalk. Tie into four bundles and put upright into a large pan of slightly salted boiling water. Cover and leave to cook.

Add the egg yolks to the vinegar and beat together. Put the bowl over a saucepan of just simmering water. Add the butter, cut into about 8 pieces, one bit at a time, whisking well until it has melted before adding the next. Keep beating until the sauce has thickened nicely and season lightly. (For fuller details see page 179.)

Test the asparagus after about 12-15 minutes to see if it is tender (cooking time varies depending on the thickness of the stems). Drain, mix the orange juice and rind into the warm hollandaise sauce and serve immediately with sea salt and pepper grinders for those who require them.

Three-in-One

Here are three dishes made from a 1 lb (450 g) bundle of asparagus – ideal
for those who must buy it and helpful to those who have a reasonable
crop in the garden but too many people for supper to enjoy it served plain.

Take the asparagus, cut 2 inches (5 cm) off the bottom of the stalks
and set these pieces to one side for the soup. Divide the rest into 2
bundles, one of 4 oz (110 g) for the two-person omelette, and the rest of
8 oz (225 g) for the flan. Keep a couple of stalks to add to the soup. Tie
the bundles separately with string, bring a pan of salted water to the boil
and simmer the asparagus, including the end pieces, for about 12-15
minutes. Strain, keeping the cooking water for the soup base.

(1) Cream of Asparagus Soup

Serves 4

cooked end pieces from 1 lb
  (450 g) bunch asparagus
water used to cook asparagus (see
  above)
black pepper

1 oz (30 g) butter
1 oz (30 g) wholemeal flour
2 whole cooked asparagus
  stalks
2½ fl oz (75 ml) single cream

Take the cooking water used to boil the asparagus, measure it and reduce
it to 1½ pints (850 ml) or slightly less by fast boiling. In batches, pour it
into the liquidizer with the cooked 2 inch (5 cm) end pieces of asparagus
and blend till smooth. You may need to sieve the purée as well,
particularly if the asparagus was shop-bought or rather large. Season with
black pepper.

Melt the butter in a saucepan, add the flour and gradually stir in the
purée. Simmer gently for about 5 minutes until thickened. Chop the 2
whole asparagus stalks, add to the pan with the cream, stir gently until
heated through but not boiling, and serve.

(2) Asparagus and Soft Cheese Omelette

Serves 2

4 oz (110 g) cooked asparagus
2 tbsp low-fat cream cheese,
  e.g. Quark
1 tbsp fresh chopped chervil

4 eggs
1 tbsp water
seasoning
1 oz (30 g) butter

Cut the asparagus into pieces about 2 inches (5 cm) long. Put them in a small non-stick saucepan with the cream cheese and the chopped chervil. In a bowl, beat the eggs with the water – this gives a lighter omelette, but on no account use milk, it does not achieve the same effect at all. Season well.

Melt the butter in a non-stick frying pan (margarine is not recommended for a first-class omelette), and when it is sizzling pour in the beaten eggs. Cook over a good heat, constantly lifting the edges to let the runny egg seep down the sides. Meanwhile, very gently heat the cream cheese and asparagus. When the omelette is nearly ready (many people prefer it slightly runny inside), spoon the asparagus mixture on to one half of it and gently slide it, that side first, halfway on to a large plate. Fold the side still in the frying pan over the asparagus and cheese filling and cut the omelette into two before serving with a salad and grilled tomatoes.

(3) Asparagus Flan

This makes a firm flan that is delicious hot and equally good cold. It comes out quite firm, so is ideal to take on the first picnic of the summer. It serves four if eaten with baked or new potatoes and salads, three if served alone.

Serves 3-4

8 oz (225 g) cooked asparagus	**Shortcrust pastry**
3 eggs	3½ oz (100 g) wholemeal flour
2½ fl. oz (75 ml) single cream	1½ oz (45 g) unbleached plain
black pepper	flour
1 oz (30 g) Cheddar cheese	2½ oz (70 g) butter
	2 tbsp cold water

Make the pastry in a food processor or by hand (see page 182). Wrap it in non-PVC clingfilm and chill it on a plate in the fridge for 30 minutes.

Beat the eggs, cream and black pepper together. On a floured board, roll out the pastry, and line a greased flan tin about 7 inches (18 cm) in diameter. The sort with a removable bottom means you can serve the cooked flan out of its tin. Arrange the asparagus pieces across the bottom and pour the cream and eggs over them.

Sprinkle with the grated Cheddar and bake in an oven preheated to Gas 5/375°F/190°C for 40 minutes.

This will freeze successfully. Cook for 30 minutes only and reheat from frozen at Gas 6/400°F/200°C.

Sole with Asparagus Sauce

Asparagus is a versatile and well flavoured vegetable. Here it makes a delicate sauce to serve with lightly poached sole fillets.

Serves 4

1 lb (450 g) asparagus
4 large or 8 small sole fillets
glass dry white wine
½ pint (300 ml) water
bayleaf

black peppercorns
2-3 tbsp natural yoghurt
squeeze lemon juice
seasoning

Trim the toughest part off the end of the asparagus stalks, then wash and cook the asparagus in boiling water for 15 minutes until really tender. Meanwhile make a light stock to cook the fish in by simmering the wine, water, bayleaf and peppercorns, plus any trimmings and skin from the sole, for 15 minutes, covered. Remove from the stove and set aside.

Drain the asparagus (keeping the stock) and liquidize it with a little of the cooking liquor to form a smooth purée. Transfer to a saucepan and stir in the yoghurt, lemon juice and seasoning to taste.

Fold each of the skinned sole fillets in on itself to form a three-layer parcel and place in a shallow dish with the fish stock. Cook in an oven preheated to Gas 5/375°F/190°C for 15-20 minutes. Pour a little of the reheated sauce on to each plate, place the sole fillet or fillets on top and serve.

If you like, you can reserve a couple of the asparagus tips per portion and include them as a garnish.

Asparagus Salad

Served cold with a vinaigrette or mayonnaise, asparagus makes a lovely summer salad. On the Continent it is often mixed with other ingredients to make an interesting hors d'oeuvre.

Serves 6

1 lb (450 g) asparagus
3 eggs
1 red pepper
Cos lettuce

mayonnaise (see page 180)
juice ½ lemon
2 tbsp fresh chopped herbs
1 tbsp capers

Tie the asparagus into bundles and cook in the normal way for 12-15 minutes. Hardboil the eggs. Grill the red pepper, turning often, until it is blistered and beginning to char and then rub the outer skin off under cold running water. Drain the asparagus, shell and quarter the eggs. Thinly slice the red pepper, which should be fairly soft now, removing the inner core and seeds.

Wash the lettuce and arrange the inner crisp leaves, torn into pieces, on an oval serving dish. Lay the asparagus in 6 bundles across the centre, with the eggs in between.

Make the mayonnaise and beat in the extra lemon juice, a little at a time, to thin it down to pouring consistency. Stir in the fresh herbs and then pour the mayonnaise over the asparagus stems, leaving the tops clear. Arrange a couple of strips of red pepper between the egg quarters, piling the rest at the ends of the dish. Chop the capers and scatter them over the eggs.

Serve with pumpernickel bread. This salad also makes a good open sandwich using pumpernickel, in which case you should slice rather than quarter the eggs and not thin the mayonnaise.

Broad Beans

Broad beans have been cultivated, according to the archaeologists, since the Bronze Age at least, some claim since the Stone Age. They were the only bean known in Europe until the other varieties like French (haricot) and runner arrived from the New World. If you grow your own, you can begin picking them in early May, although the main crop are ready a bit later. In either case they are the first of the garden beans to arrive in the kitchen and you can soon become overwhelmed by the quantity and find yourself racking your brains for new ways to serve them.

If you have the patience, it is a good idea to peel the tough white skin off the beans after cooking to reveal the bright green flesh underneath, especially with the larger ones. Unfortunately those sold in greengrocers are often too large and past their best, suitable only for soups or purées. When you do find the smaller ones on sale it is really worth snapping them up there and then and taking the opportunity to serve them in some new and different ways.

Estimating quantities is difficult – you usually end up with about 6-8 oz (170-225 g) of shelled beans to every unshelled pound (450 g), although this varies considerably. Always buy or pick a little extra, you can freeze any that are left over. Stored unshelled in the fridge they keep for about four to five days, though all beans are obviously better the fresher they are. *Very* young ones can be boiled in the pod and eaten whole.

Broad Bean and Basil Soup

This will convert even those who aren't too keen on broad beans, and is also quite a useful way of using ones that have grown a little too large for eating plain. If you don't have any fresh basil, don't use dried which is too bitter for this dish, but substitute chervil or savory or, as a last resort, parsley.

Serves 4

1 lb (450 g) shelled broad beans	1 tbsp fresh chopped basil
½ medium onion	black pepper
1 small clove garlic	1dsp lemon juice
½ oz (15 g) butter	1 tbsp natural yoghurt
1½ pints (850 ml) chicken stock	

Slice the onion and sweat it gently in the butter with the garlic for a few minutes. Add the beans and stock with the fresh basil and bring to the boil. Simmer gently, covered, for about 10 minutes or until the beans are tender. Remove half-a-dozen and set aside for a garnish. Liquidize the soup and then strain it through a sieve to remove the slightly tough white outer skins of the beans.

Return to the saucepan and season with black pepper. Reheat with a squeeze of lemon juice, stir in the natural yoghurt and serve sprinkled with the reserved beans, outer skins removed and divided in half.

Broad Bean and Asparagus Salad

A lovely way to enjoy the first vegetables of summer is to combine these two in a salad. If you are lucky enough to grow your own, you should pick the beans when young and small, and choose the thinnest asparagus stems. When you have to buy the ingredients, you may need to be more persistent to get the right quality, but it is still achievable.

Serves 4

12 oz (335 g) shelled broad beans	French dressing made with
1 lb (450 g) asparagus	lemon juice instead of vinegar
2 tbsp fresh chopped parsley	(see page 181)
black pepper	2 slices lemon

Simmer the beans in slightly salted water for 7-10 minutes until tender, then drain and refresh under cold running water. Small ones can be left as they are, but it is worth removing the outer white skin from larger ones. Put on one side. Cut off the ends of the asparagus, then tie the stems together and simmer upright with a lid on in slightly salted water until cooked, which will take about 10 minutes. Drain and refresh. (You may cook the cut-off ends as well and keep them and the cooking liquid for a soup, see page 25).

Dry the beans and asparagus on kitchen paper, cut the asparagus stems into 1 inch (2.5cm) lengths and transfer both vegetables to a shallow bowl. Scatter the parsley over and season with black pepper. Pour on the French dressing. Mix gently and serve decorated with a couple of twists of thinly sliced lemon.

Broad Bean Stuffed Tomatoes

I rather like the nutty taste of the shredded outer skins of the beans in this recipe, but if yours are on the old side you would do best to peel it off (in which case allow extra weight of beans to start with).

Serves 4

8 oz (225 g) shelled broad beans	½ oz (15 g) butter
4 reasonably large tomatoes	black pepper
(about 12 oz/335 g)	

Slice the tomatoes in half widthways and scoop out the pips with a teaspoon. Cook the beans in simmering water for about 15 minutes until tender, then drain and purée with the butter and lots of black pepper. Pile the purée into the tomato shells, and bake in a preheated oven at Gas 6/400°F/200°C for 10-15 minutes until the tonato shells are just soft, but not disintegrating. Serve immediately.

Broad Bean Lemon Tartlets

This is a delicious way of serving young broad beans. You have to peel off the outer skin of the beans before filling the pastry cases, but this doesn't take too long and the result is well worth the effort. They can be served as a starter, or a filling side-dish together with another light vegetable or a salad instead of potatoes.

Serves 6

12 oz (335 g) shelled broad beans	**Shortcrust pastry**
1 oz (30 g) butter	4½ oz (125 g) wholemeal flour
1 oz (30 g) plain flour	1½ oz (45 g) plain flour
less than ½ pint (300 ml) milk	3 oz (85 g) butter
1 tbsp fresh chopped parsley	1-2 tbsp cold water
1 lemon	
black pepper	

First prepare the pastry shells. Make the shortcrust dough in the usual way (see page 182). Roll it out thinly and cut circles to fit 6 shallow tartlet tins of 4 inches (10 cm) diameter. Grease the tins lightly and line them with the pastry, then chill for 30 minutes.

Simmer the broad beans until tender, then refresh under cold water to halt the cooking and peel off the pale outer skins using a small knife and your fingers. Set aside.

Make a white sauce in the usual way (page 178), stirring in only enough milk to make it really thick but smooth, then stir in the cooked beans, fresh parsley and grated rind of the lemon. Finish with a squeeze of lemon juice and some freshly ground black pepper.

Bake the pastry shells blind for 15 minutes at Gas 6/400°F/200°C, then remove the greaseproof paper and bake a further 5 minutes. Fill with the hot broad bean and lemon mixture and serve. If you prepare this in advance, don't fill the pastry shells too far ahead or they will go soggy. Once you have assembled them, warm through in an oven preheated to Gas 6/400°F/200°C for 10 minutes, covered with silver foil to prevent the sauce from forming a dry skin.

Lamb

As a result of modern rearing methods, the traditional British season for lamb (from spring to early autumn) does not apply so strictly as it once did. However, those reared in spring and killed during the summer have been feeding on new grass, which gives them a better flavour than the autumn-lambing varieties. Early summer is therefore a good time to pick up a whole British lamb for your freezer. This is an economical way of buying it – so long as you can think of enough ways of cooking the various joints! All too often the popular cuts like the legs get used up, leaving bags of chops or joints like the breast because you can't find the inspiration to cook them interestingly. To help avoid this it is useful to have some recipes that ring the changes from an endless diet of grilled chops and traditional roasts.

If you are purchasing in bulk, get the butcher to cut the carcass up for you, and see that the different cuts are clearly labelled before you freeze them. It is important, too, to make sure you wrap them up well, to prevent them from being spoilt by freezer burn.

Technically, a lamb is any young sheep killed while it is under a year old – beyond this it becomes mutton. Milk-fed lamb, which many people find rather fatty and tasteless, is only a month or so old, and is born in winter and raised under cover on milk. However, most of the lamb we eat in Britain is killed at between three and nine months old, those of three to four months (around 22 lb or 10 kg) being the best. In general, modern lamb is bred to have less fat than previously, and needs to be more carefully cooked to keep it succulent. Mountain lambs, such as those from Wales which have a more active life roaming the hills, may have a slightly less tender flesh but undeniably taste better as well.

When serving lamb in the form of a plain roast joint, spice it up with some Fresh

Mint Chutney. For other ways of using lamb, see the recipes for
Courgettes Stuffed with Minced Lamb, Cornish Apple and Lamb Pie,
and Moussaka.

Lamb in Minty Mayonnaise

If you want to serve something more original than sliced ham and
Coronation chicken for a cold buffet, try this delicious lamb and mint
recipe.

Serves 6-8

1 leg or shoulder of lamb
  (4½ lb/2 kg)
2 cloves garlic
sunflower oil for roasting

½ pint (300 ml) or more homemade mayonnaise (see page 180)
1-2 tbsp hot water
2-3 tbsp fresh chopped mint
few mint leaves for decoration

Make small incisions in the outside of the lamb. Slice the garlic into thin
slivers and push into the flesh. Slow roast in a little hot oil at
Gas 4/350°F/180°C, allowing 25 minutes to the lb (450 g) and 25
minutes extra, basting occasionally.

When completely cold cut the meat off the bone in thick pieces and
divide into bite-sized chunks. Put the mayonnaise in a fairly large bowl
and add a tablespoon of very hot water, beat well and add a little more if
necessary until it is of a coating consistency. Stir in the lamb and
chopped mint, arrange piled up on a flat plate and decorate with a few
whole mint leaves. Refrigerate until required, then serve surrounded by a
ring of brown rice.

Loin of Lamb with Coriander

This is a delicious and easy way to liven up a piece of roast lamb. Once
cooked, the coriander seeds go quite soft, so you don't have to worry
about picking them out before eating. Ask your butcher to bone the
joint, if this is not already done, but not tie it. Boned shoulder of lamb
can be used instead. Allow about 8 oz (225 g) of boneless meat per head,
and remember that it shrinks slightly while cooking.

Serves 4

2 lb (900 g) boned loin of lamb
1 tbsp coriander seeds
3 cloves garlic
3 tbsp sunflower oil
black pepper

Gravy
1 dsp-1 tbsp wholemeal flour
½ glass white wine
¼-½ pint (150-300 ml) stock

Crush the coriander seeds with the garlic in a mortar and pestle (or pulverize the seeds in the corner of a clean tea towel with a rolling pin and crush the garlic separately). Spread the mixture on the inside of the lamb joint, roll up and tie at intervals along the joint to prevent it from unrolling while cooking. Put a small roasting tin containing a little oil in the oven while you preheat it to Gas 7/425°F/220°C.

Season the lamb with black pepper and put it in the hot oil. Roast at this high temperature for 20 minutes, then lower the heat to Gas 5/375°F/190°C and allow 20 minutes to the pound. This will result in slightly pink lamb. If you like yours well done allow another 15-20 minutes.

Remove from the oven and keep warm. Drain the fat off the top of the juices in the pan, scrape the crusty meaty bits with a wooden spoon and stir in a little flour. Gradually add the stock and wine, boil well, test for seasoning and serve in a warmed sauceboat. Carve the lamb into thick slices.

Lamb Gosht Maurya

Those who love Indian food will find it worth buying the individual spices needed to produce the variety of flavours essential to an authentic curry. Personally I get great satisfaction from making a real curry (as opposed to one with curry powder), taking a bit of this and a bit of that. When in Singapore I brought a host of whole spices really cheaply, along with a solid stone pestle and mortar. In Britain you can find these in specialist shops, but ready-ground ones are acceptable so long as they are not too old.

In this dish you can still taste the sweetness of the lamb, despite the different spices that have been used. I find super-hot curries overwhelm the basic ingredients, which seems rather pointless.

Serves 4

1¾-2 lb (785-900 g) shoulder
    of lamb
1 medium onion
2 cloves garlic
2 inches (5 cm) fresh ginger
3-4 tbsp ghee or clarified
    butter or 5 tbsp sunflower oil
1 inch (2.5 cm) piece cinnamon
2 bayleaves
5 cloves

5 cardamom pods
1½ oz (45 g) cumin seeds
1 tsp chilli powder
1½ tsp turmeric
1½ tsp ground cumin
1 tsp ground coriander
1 small tub (150 g) natural yoghurt
3 oz (85 g) ground almonds
7½ fl.oz (225 ml) water

Trim the fat from the lamb and dice the lean meat – you should end up with a minimum of 1¼ lb (550 g). Chop the onion. Peel the garlic cloves and ginger, chop them roughly and pound to a paste in a pestle and mortar (or put through a garlic crusher, adding the bits left behind as well).

Heat the fat – ghee gives an authentic flavour and can be bought tinned in Asian shops, but sunflower oil will do. Add the cinnamon, bayleaves, cloves, whole cardamom pods and cumin seeds with the onion. Fry, stirring, until the onion is golden brown.

Remove from the heat and add the garlic and ginger, chilli, turmeric, ground cumin and coriander. Cook gently for a minute or so to fry the spices. Stir in the yoghurt (lightly beaten to break it down somewhat), ground almonds and water. Mix well, bring to the boil and simmer for 15-20 minutes until the fat has risen to the surface. Be careful to keep the heat quite low, or the sauce will stick.

Add the diced lamb and cook for a further 30-35 minutes over a low heat. Serve with brown rice and a side dish like the recipe for Spicy Aubergines.

Lamb Wellington Noisettes

If you only have enough chops left from your big freezer buy to serve one each, it can look a bit mean on the plate. I quite often find that a single lamb chop, unless it's very thick, is not enough for those with large appetites. This is a clever way to turn just one chop into a substantial meal – the richness of the pâté plus the pastry make a very ample serving.

Serves 6

6 lamb chops, about ¾ inch (2 cm) thick	2-3 tbsp sherry seasoning
1 small onion	3 oz (85 g) button mushrooms
4 oz (110 g) chicken livers	7½ oz (195 g) packet puff pastry
1 oz (30 g) butter	beaten egg

Bone the chops and cut any large slabs of fat from them. Finely chop the onion. Sauté the chicken livers in the butter with the onion until browned, add the sherry and seasoning, then purée the mixture in a food processor or mash by hand. Leave to cool while you finely chop the mushrooms, then mix them in.

Roll out the pastry thinly and cut it into 6 squares. Spread one side of each chop with the pâté and put the chop, pâté side down, on to a pastry square. Fold the sides over, cutting off as much excess pastry as possible and seal by brushing with water where the edges touch. Turn over so the join is underneath. Make a small hole in the top of each parcel, decorate if you like with a pastry leaf or two, and brush the whole surface with beaten egg.

Bake in an oven preheated to Gas 6/400°F/200°C for 40 minutes. Instead of potatoes, which the pastry can replace, serve two large dishes of vegetables like carrots and broccoli.

Irish Stew

You may be surprised to find this familiar recipe here. *I* am surprised by how few people know how to make it, or appreciate how good it is. It uses the cheapest cut of meat, scrag end (a part it is hard to know what to do with), although you can make it with middle neck chops if you prefer. The broth should be thick and creamy, not all watery. Traditionally only potatoes and onions are added, but I find pearl barley is an excellent addition and some chopped parsley thrown in at the end brightens the stew up.

This was one of my favourite dishes when a child, no doubt partly because all the finger-licking gnawing of the bones appealed to the piggy side of my nature !

Serves 6

3½ lb (1.55 kg) scrag end or 3 lb (1.35 kg) middle neck chops
2½ lb (1.1 kg) potatoes
2 lb (900 g) onions
bayleaf

water or meat stock to cover
seasoning
2-3 tbsp pearl barley
2 tbsp fresh chopped parsley

Trim some of the excess fat from the meat and cut into chops or serving pieces. Cut the potatoes into thick ¼ inch (½ cm) slices (you may leave the peel on if you wish). Slice the onions thickly. Put a layer of potato at the bottom of a large saucepan or casserole, then a layer of onion and follow this with half the lamb. Season well and repeat, then finish with a layer of potato. Add the bayleaf and pour enough stock in at the side to just come up to the top layer, then bring slowly to the boil. Leave to simmer very gently for 2 hours, adding the pearl barley and pushing it down into the stew after the first hour.

Scatter with the parsley and serve very hot with a simply prepared vegetable like cabbage cooked gently in butter for a really economical meal.

If you wish to cut down on the fattiness of this dish, cook it for 15 minutes less, then leave it to go cold overnight. The fat will solidify on top and can be easily removed. Reheat and serve.

Lamb and Runner Bean Casserole

This is a good supper dish, easily prepared and not needing too long a
cooking time. Portions are generous and all you need to accompany it are
some new potatoes.

Serves 4

8 boneless loin of lamb chops
1 medium onion
8 tomatoes
2 cloves garlic
2 tbsp sunflower oil
¼ pint (150 ml) white wine
2 tbsp wholemeal flour

1 pint (550 ml) lamb or chicken
    stock
1 tbsp fresh chopped basil or
    pinch dried
bayleaf
seasoning
1 lb (450 g) runner beans

Trim most of the fat off the chops and slice the onion. Peel the tomatoes
(dropping them in boiling water for 10 seconds and then into cold
loosens the skins), and chop them. Heat the oil in a flameproof casserole
and sauté the onion, garlic and chops over a fairly high heat, turning the
chops once so they are browned on both sides. Remove the meat and set
it to one side.

Stir in the wine and reduce it over a medium heat, scraping the
bottom of the dish with a spoon. Stir in the flour and gradually add the
stock until it is well blended. Return the lamb chops to the dish with the
tomatoes, basil, bayleaf and seasoning. Simmer, covered, for 45 minutes.

Slice the beans in the usual way and add them to the casserole. Return
to a simmer and cook a further 10 minutes until the beans are ready and
their flavour has permeated the dish.

Lemons

Although lemons are now available all the year round, they are at their
cheapest in early summer, becoming more expensive in the autumn.
They are grown anywhere which is frost free with a warm sunny climate,
but do not thrive so well in the tropics, where you find limes taking over
instead. The lemons sold in Britain come mainly from France, Spain,
Israel and California.

Gone are the days when you bought one or two lemons in your weekly
shopping. They are now sold in fives or even tens by market stalls for
remarkably low prices, and sometimes you may find yourself faced with
what seems an excess in your kitchen. But lemons have a multitude of
uses, and since they keep for a couple of weeks in the bottom of the fridge

you can never have too many. There are numerous recipes which feature lemon juice as one of the major ingredients, a selection of which I give here.

You can also, of course, cut them into slices and wedges to serve with drinks, fish and fried food (incidentally always cut a wedge if you intend people to add a squeeze of juice – no one can squeeze a thin slice). A squeeze of lemon juice is a good substitute for salt as a flavour enhancer for many dishes, to be added to personal taste at the table. The zest – the very outermost skin – can be scraped off with a special lemon zester, or pared with a potato peeler and finely shredded to give a delicious and subtle flavour when added to meat dishes, cakes and puddings. In any recipe that calls for sour cream, you can simply add a squeeze of lemon juice to ordinary cream, stir and leave to stand for a few minutes before using.

Note that despite their similarity, limes, which often feature in recipes from the tropics, are much stronger than lemons as well as having a different flavour. Do not be confused by the word *limón* in recipes from South America. In Spain it means lemon, but in the tropics it describes a lime.

For other ways of using lemons see the recipes for Tabbouleh and for Broad Bean and Lemon Tartlets. Lemon appears in sauces, too – see Greek Brussels Sprouts – and as a substitute for vinegar in French dressing (see for example Broad Bean and Asparagus Salad, French Beans
Mimosa, Avocado with Strawberry Sauce and Leeks Vinaigrette).

Greek Lemon Soup (Avgolemono)

This is one of my favourite soups, though I have never eaten it in Greece, only in the more unusual Greek restaurants in London. When I first came to make it at home I found it surprisingly easy, and of course very cheap. However, you must use good homemade chicken stock – a bouillon cube alone won't do here, although you can add one to enrich your stock if you decide, after tasting, that it isn't strong enough.

Serves 4

1½ lemons	white or black pepper
2¼ pints (1.3 litres) chicken stock	celery leaves, Continental
1½ oz (45 g) rice	parsley or English parsley to
2 egg yolks	garnish

If you are using brown rice, it is best to cook it in advance until almost ready or you will find the soup gets a bit scummy. I prefer white rice, which is lighter, for this dish.

Bring the stock to the boil and add the rice (part-cooked if brown) and boil until tender. Squeeze the juice from the lemons. Beat the egg yolks in a bowl and pour most of the juice over them. Beat well again. Add a soup ladle of the hot soup to the bowl, blend it in well and then return the whole lot to the pan. (If you add the egg yolks direct to the soup they tend to curdle – or rather, scramble.) Season with the pepper and continue to cook over a gentle heat, stirring well, until the soup starts to thicken. Again, don't let it boil or the eggs will cook. Taste, and add the rest of the lemon juice if necessary.

Serve sprinkled with a few freshly chopped celery leaves, or a little of the flat-leaved Continental parsley available from Greek greengrocers. English will do, but doesn't really have the same delicately pungent flavour.

Lemon Mousse with Pineapple Surprise

I now make most of my mousses using natural yoghurt instead of whipped double cream – cheaper and much healthier. The taste is slightly sharper, but not noticeably different from the classic version. In this recipe I have made a well in the middle of the mousse and filled it with pineapple, then covered the top with slices of lemon so that the contents come as an unexpected surprise.

Do not add the pineapple more than an hour before serving, as the fresh juices contain an enzyme which destroys the setting effect of gelatine and also returns whipped egg whites to liquid.

Serves 4-6

2½ large juicy lemons
3 eggs
2-3 tbsp clear honey
0.4 oz (11 g) sachet gelatine

small tub (150 g) natural yoghurt
½ fresh pineapple (8 oz/225 g
    after trimming)

Separate the eggs into two big bowls. Setting the half lemon aside for decoration, grate the rind from the remaining two and add it to the yolks. Squeeze the juice from the same two lemons into a small saucepan and add the honey. Sprinkle the gelatine all over the surface, then set the pan on one side for a few minutes to allow the gelatine to sponge.

Beat the yolks and rind together till pale and creamy. Heat the gelatine very gently until both it and the honey have completely dissolved in the lemon juice, then gradually add to the yolks, beating all the time. Stir in the yoghurt until well blended and chill until the contents are on the point of setting.

Meanwhile prepare a 1¼ pint (700 ml) soufflé dish, by stapling 2 widths of folded greaseproof paper tightly around the outside of the rim to provide a barrier when you pour in the mixture. (I find stapling the pieces together much less fiddly than tying them.) Whisk the egg whites until stiff and fold them into the mousse. Pour the mixture into the soufflé dish, having first placed a Worcestershire sauce bottle or something of a similar diameter in the middle (make sure the outside is clean !) Chill until set and then loosen round the bottle with a knife before gently lifting it out.

Trim the pineapple and cut it into cubes (you may sprinkle it with a little liqueur like Grand Marnier if you wish). Cut the half lemon into thin slices and halve these. Shortly before serving, fill the hole in the centre of the mousse with the pineapple chunks, then cover them with overlapping slices of lemon.

Should you decide to omit the pineapple and just make a plain mousse, you will not need to staple the paper round the edge of the dish, as the mousse will not come over the rim.

Uncooked Lemon Cheesecake

I have used natural yoghurt instead of double cream again here, with surprising success. Surprising, because one would expect the difference in flavour to be quite marked in the end dish, but my guess is that if you served this to someone who had only ever eaten cream-based cheesecake or mousse, they would never even notice.

Serves 8

2 large lemons
4 oz (110 g) wholemeal digestive
   biscuits
2 oz (55 g) butter
2-3 tbsp clear honey
0.4 oz (11 g) packet gelatine

3 large eggs
7 oz (195 g) low-fat cream
   cheese
1 small tub (150 g) natural
   yoghurt

Crush the biscuits well with a rolling pin on a large board. Melt the butter in a saucepan and add the biscuit crumbs, stirring well until thoroughly mixed in. Transfer to an 8 inch (20 cm) diameter cake tin with a removable bottom, and press down well with your hand to form a firm base. Put into the fridge for the butter to harden.

Wash the lemons and grate the rind, then halve them and squeeze out the juice. Put the juice in a small saucepan with the honey and sprinkle the gelatine over the surface. Leave to sponge. Separate the eggs, putting the whites in one large mixing bowl and the yolks in another. Whisk the yolks well (using an electric whisk if you have one) until pale and creamy. Beat in the cream cheese, yoghurt and lemon rind.

Heat the lemon juice in the pan very gently until the gelatine and honey have dissolved. On no account let it boil. Cool slightly, stir gradually into the yolks, beating well, and transfer to the fridge. After about 10-15 minutes the mixture will be getting quite thick, at which point whisk the egg whites stiffly and fold them in. Pour on top of the biscuit base in the cake tin and leave to set for several hours in the fridge.

To serve, carefully push the base up through the sides of the tin and transfer to a plate.

Pickled Lemons

If you eat curries regularly this is an excellent pickle to make to go with them. By the time it is ready to use the lemons are quite soft, and you can eat the rind and everything.

6 lemons
about 1 pint (550 ml) distilled
   vinegar (clear)
2½ tsp ground mixed spice

1½ tsp turmeric
4 tbsp sea salt
dash Tabasco

Wipe the outsides of the lemons well. Holding them on a plate to catch the juice, quarter them and cut into small chunks, removing the pips. Pack into two smallish Kilner jars with clip-down tops. Pour a little vinegar on to the plate, add the spices, salt and Tabasco and mix well, then pour over the lemons. Cover with vinegar and close the jar tightly.

Leave the jar in a fairly warm place, either an airing cupboard, by the stove or above the motor of a fridge or freezer. Shake the jars once every so often. After a few weeks the skins will be soft (there is no harm in opening the jar to test for this). The jars should then be transferred to the larder or a cupboard for 6 months before using.

Lift out with a slotted spoon or drain a few chunks in a sieve before putting in a small dish on the table.

Preserved Lemons

These are milder than the pickled lemons above, as they are preserved in oil rather than vinegar. They are common in the Middle East. Try them with a dish like Tabbouleh or with Stuffed Aubergines.

6 lemons
4 tbsp sea salt

2 tsp paprika
sunflower or safflower oil

Halve the lemons lengthways and cut the halves into slices. Leave for 24 hours in a colander sprinkled with the sea salt, then pat dry and fill two smallish Kilner jars with the slices, adding a little paprika between some of the layers. Carefully cover with the oil, seal and leave for 3-4 weeks before using.

Real Lemonade

In the days before cans and sodastreams and fizzy drinks, people used to make their own soft drinks and many of these are much more refreshing than the sticky-sweet ones that line our supermarket walls. Here I give two recipes, a traditional one made by drawing the lemon taste out with boiling water, and a more modern one made with a liquidizer. Personally I go for the latter, which has a much stronger flavour, but it all depends on individual preference.

I have substituted honey for sugar in the first recipe – you can adjust the sweetening to your taste if necessary. In the second, since it is unheated, honey will not dissoslve, so you should use sugar. Make sure you use juicy lemons with unblemished, firm skins.

Method 1

3 lemons
1½ tbsp clear honey

2 pints (1.1 litres) water
few sprigs of mint

Wipe the lemons, halve and dice them on a small board, tipping any juice with the lemon dice into a plastic or metal measuring jug. Add the honey. Boil a kettle of water and pour about 2 pints (1.1 litres) over the lemons. Leave to infuse for 20 minutes or a little longer, then strain into a glass jug and chill for 2 hours. Serve with a thin slice of lemon and a sprig of mint in each glass.

This makes an almost clear drink.

Method 2

2 lemons
2 pints (1.1 litres) water

1-2 level tbsp sugar

Wipe the lemons and halve them, then cut each half into 4 pieces. Put these in the liquidizer and pour in the water. Process for about 15-20 seconds then strain into a glass jug. Stir the sugar into the liquid in the jug and chill.

This makes a cloudy drink with a strong lemon taste, for a weaker flavour add extra water at the end. Do not overprocess or the skin will leave a rather bitter taste.

Mint

Mint is a delicious and unmistakable herb to use in cooking. Even over the long dark years when the British shut fresh herbs out of their kitchens, except for chopped parsley in a gluey white sauce, mint was still used when cooking vegetables, particularly new potatoes and tiny garden peas. A tip I picked up from a half-Russian friend is to cram a whole bunch of mint into the saucepan with your potatoes, instead of the odd leaf or two we timid British tend to use. This way not only does the flavour permeate the potatoes, but the wonderful aroma wafts up through the house. Young mint leaves are also good added to a dressed green salad.

Mint grows like crazy anywhere it is planted and spreads fast, although it isn't very successful in window boxes (easier to buy bunches fresh from the greengrocer). It is necessary to pick it regularly to prevent it from taking over your garden and it is easy, but a pity, to let the surplus go to waste. English mint becomes tougher as autumn approaches, and the first frosts usually kill it off, but in early summer it is at its best.

There are lots of varieties, all giving faintly different tastes – round slightly furry apple mint is very juicy while spearmint (also known as lamb or pea mint and recognizable by its pointed leaves) is the type most commonly found in greengrocers, since it doesn't wilt as quickly once picked. Mint is widely used in Middle Eastern cooking, often dried, and it goes very well with lemon juice – as in the recipe here for Tabbouleh.

If you grow your own mint, obviously just pick it as and when you need it, remembering that the tips and uppermost leaves are the most tender. If buying bunched mint, you can keep it fresh for a few days by stripping off the extreme lower leaves and standing it in a jar of water, stalks down. Pick off any brown leaves as they appear, However, it is best to use it as soon as possible and the recipes here should help you avoid having to waste any.

For additional ways of using this herb, see Lamb in Minty Mayonnaise, Chilled Strawberry Soup, Courgettes Stuffed with Minced Lamb, Cold Cucumber Soup, Tomatoes Stuffed with Minty Peas, Aubergine and Yoghurt Salad, Leeks Vinaigrette and Rhubarb and Mint Jelly.

Tabbouleh

I have yet to meet anyone who doesn't take to this Middle Eastern salad the first time they try it. In the authentic version the cracked wheat, also known as burgul, should be mixed with generous quantities of fresh chopped mint and parsley, as well as lots of lemon juice and black pepper. Unfortunately insipid versions are sometimes served up, often in London restaurants that are too busy following food fashions to concentrate on ingredients. I once had one totally devoid of herbs and stained orange-red with tomato sauce. Here is the real thing, which is a good way to enjoy the taste of really fresh mint. Serve either as a starter or as part of a summer lunch with fish, lamb or other salads and dips.

Cracked wheat, also known as burgul, is available from wholefood shops and Middle Eastern grocery stores. If you can get the flat-leaved Continental parsley, use it in this dish for a really authentic flavour.

Serves 4

4 tbsp fresh chopped mint
8 oz (225 g) cracked wheat
1 medium onion
6-8 tbsp fresh chopped parsley

4 tbsp olive oil
4 tbsp lemon juice
seasoning
2-3 lettuce leaves

Soak the cracked wheat in cold water for 30 minutes. Finely chop the onion. When the soaking time is up, drain the swollen wheat into a fine sieve, then tip it into a clean tea towel and squeeze as much moisture out as possible. Empty it into a bowl and add the chopped onion, squeezing the mixture in your hands to crush the onion and let the juices out. This is rather messy, but really extracts the flavour. Wash your hands well afterwards.

Stir in the remaining ingredients and leave for at least an hour to allow the flavours to develop, then taste to see if you need to add a little more of anything, before piling on to lettuce leaves and serving.

You may include a little finely chopped cucumber and chopped, deseeded tomatoes as well, but do not mix them in until the last moment or they will make the salad rather soggy.

Mint and Cucumber Yoghurt Salad

I have always found this to be a very popular salad, as it tastes cool and refreshing without having that slightly sharp flavour that some people dislike in plain yoghurt. It brings out the flavour of mint at its best.

Serves 4-6

2-3 tbsp fresh chopped mint
1 large cucumber
4 spring onions

2 small cartons (2 x 150 g)
   natural yoghurt
pinch paprika

Top and tail the cucumber. Pare off the skin in alternate strips with a potato peeler, so you leave some of the bright green skin behind. Slice fairly thinly and cut the slices into matchstick shreds. Slice the onions thinly and mix them with the cucumber, mint and yoghurt. Chill for about 30 minutes, but not much longer or the cucumber starts to produce rather a lot of liquid. Sprinkle with paprika and serve.

Mint Julep

This drink evokes pictures of *Gone With the Wind*, of a southern belle lounging on the verandah, sipping from a tall ice-cold glass. Doubtless no self-respecting Southern belle was allowed to drink such hard liquor, but the image is appealing ! Try it for yourself on a hot summer's day.

Serves 8

small handful mint sprigs
soda water

1¼ pints (700 ml) bourbon whisky

Put the washed mint sprigs and a little soda water into a medium-sized jug. Mash these up well with a wooden spoon and then pour on the bourbon. Chill well to allow the mint flavour to permeate, then pour into highball glasses of ½ pint (300 ml) capacity and top up with soda water. If you wish, stir in a level teaspoon of sugar per glass.

Mint Tea

This is drunk all over the Middle East and North Africa and is wonderfully refreshing. I first tasted it in a merchant's room in the carpet town of Kairouan in Tunisia, where I had gone to buy a rug. Invited upstairs, mint tea was served and pleasantries exchanged before we got down to the serious business of haggling. Whenever I taste it now, it always brings back memories of that afternoon in the cool dim room with the sunlight filtering through the carved window lattices, shuttering out the noise of the bazaar and scents from the hot streets below.

The best mint to use is the spearmint variety, with pointed leaves. Green tea can be bought in Chinese supermarkets and some wholefood stores.

medium bunch fresh mint or a
    handful unchopped dried mint
    leaves

1½ tbsp green tea
1½-2 pints (850 ml-1.1 litres)
    boiling water

Strip the mint leaves from the stalks, until you have a handful. Bring the water to the boil, rinse out the teapot with a swill of boiling water to warm it, add the mint and green tea plus a little sugar to taste if you like. Traditionally this is served quite sweet, but it is good without sugar too. Pour on the boiling water. Leave to infuse for 5-8 minutes and serve in glasses or small cups.

Fresh Mint Chutney

This is an Indian recipe. Most chutneys there are made and eaten fresh, rather than being cooked and bottled as in England. This one is especially good as an accompaniment to lamb, in place of mint sauce which all too often is so sharp that it entirely ruins the taste of the lamb, flooding it with a bath of vinegar.

A food processor is ideal for making this chutney, otherwise chop everything very finely first and beat together by hand.

handful fresh mint leaves   1 green chilli
1 small onion   pinch salt
1 cooking apple   few tbsp water

Finely chop the onion, mint leaves and peeled and cored apple, in a food processor if you have one. Deseed the chilli, wearing rubber gloves to protect your hands, and add to the chopped ingredients until fiery enough for your taste. Add the salt, and beat in just enough water to achieve a smooth paste. If you like, you may add a little desiccated coconut, ground fine, to take some of the hotness out of the chutney. You may also include a little sugar if you wish.

This chutney does not keep and should be eaten the same day.

Spinach

Spinach was introduced to Europe by the Arabs, who probably took it from the Persians (the Persian word for it being *aspanakh*). Certainly it is a common ingredient in much Middle Eastern cooking. It has been grown in England since the sixteenth century but was originally used only for medicinal purposes, as a mild laxative. Although it is available much of the year the best season is early May, when the new growth is ready for harvesting.

Home-grown spinach is a very useful vegetable to have in the kitchen garden, since you can pick as much as you need and the plant quickly produces new leaves. As young leaves are obviously more tender than old, you need to pick it regularly to enjoy it at its best, and in high season this can lead to rather a surplus. However, you don't need to serve it just plainly cooked – you can soon use it up by chopping and puréeing it and by transforming it into soups, soufflés or salads, serving it with eggs or mixing it in with pasta.

Bear in mind when picking or buying that because of its high water content, 1 lb (450 g) of fresh spinach reduces to only about 8 oz (225 g) when cooked. Depending on the soil it is grown in, it can be rather gritty so always wash it well in two or more changes of cold water. The stalks if large should be torn out, but don't discard them as they make a very good vegetable dish simmered gently on their own. Cook the leaves in a pan with no added water – that left on the leaves from the washing should be sufficient, but turn occasionally to ensure they are not sticking to the bottom. After draining, put the cooked leaves on a tough china plate, lay another on top and press hard between your hands to extract all surplus water.

Bought spinach wilts very quickly and should be used up fast. Don't bother to buy it at all if it looks old and limp. Ideally the leaves should be squeaky crisp. In a plastic bag at the bottom of the fridge, leaves as fresh as this will last a couple of days.

Some people find the taste a little strong when served plain, and indeed the older leaves can leave a rather metallic coating in the mouth, in which case it is better to serve it puréed with a little cream or velouté sauce.

See also Salmon Steaks Florentine.

Spinach and Almond Soup

Although the spinach should be fresh for this soup, it doesn't have to be made from the very young leaves – keep those for a salad. It is a light soup heralding summer eating, thickened only with ground almonds. Try to use homemade chicken stock, although a bouillon cube will do.

Serves 4

1 lb (450 g) spinach	1 pint (550 ml) chicken stock
1 medium onion	bayleaf
1 oz (30 g) butter	½ pint (300 ml) milk
2 oz (55 g) ground almonds	seasoning

Chop the onion roughly and sauté it for 5 minutes in the butter in a sauce-pan large enough to hold the spinach. Wash the spinach thoroughly in a sinkful of water, snapping off the thicker stems. Put it into the saucepan and turn a few times with a spoon, cover and cook for a few minutes, then stir in the ground almonds. Pour on the stock and add the bayleaf, bring to the boil and simmer, covered, for 10 minutes.

Liquidize and return to a saucepan with the milk. Season (do not add salt if you have used a stock cube), and simmer for another 5 minutes over a low heat. Serve with wholemeal bread.

Spinach Salad

Make sure the spinach is as tender and fresh as possible for this easy-to-assemble salad.

Serves 4-6

8 oz (225 g) spinach
2 eggs
3 rashers back bacon

2 oz (55 g) unsalted peanuts
French dressing (see page 181)

Wash the spinach well in plenty of cold water and snap off the stems. Tear the leaves gently into pieces and put them in the salad bowl. Hardboil the eggs, de-rind the bacon and grill it till crisp.

Shell and chop the eggs, cut the bacon into bite-sized pieces. Mix with the spinach and peanuts and toss in the French dressing at the last minute.

Spinach and Cream Cheese Ramekins

These make a good starter surrounded by a fresh tomato sauce. Use ricotta cheese or a low-fat cream cheese like Quark.

Serves 4

1 lb (450 g) cooked or frozen
   spinach
4 oz (110 g) low-fat cream cheese
pinch grated nutmeg
seasoning
1 egg
squeeze lemon juice
½ oz (15 g) butter
few sprigs parsley for garnish

Tomato sauce

12 oz (335 g) ripe tomatoes
½ small onion
2 tbsp olive oil
1 tsp tomato purée
bayleaf
parsley stalks
7½ fl. oz (225 ml) chicken stock
seasoning

To make the ramekins, put everything except the butter and parsley into a food processor and purée it. If you have to do it by hand, chop the spinach very finely indeed and beat it into the other ingredients. Rub the inside of 4 ramekins with the butter and then fill them with the spinach mixture, smoothing the tops. Put the ramekins into a bain marie (a roasting tin is fine) in an oven preheated to Gas 4/350°F/180°C. Pour in boiling water from the kettle so that it comes half-way up the sides of the ramekins and cook for 30 minutes, covered with a sheet of foil.

Meanwhile make the sauce. Loosen the skins of the tomatoes by dropping them in boiling water for the count of 10, then into cold, and peel them. Halve each one and squeeze it in your hand to remove the pips and excess moisture. Put the chopped onion (about a tablespoon) into the hot oil and cook gently till soft. Then add all the other sauce ingredients, cover and simmer for 10 minutes. Remove the bayleaf and parsley stalks and liquidize or sieve. Taste for seasoning.

Check to see the ramekins are firm to the touch then, holding them in an oven glove, invert each one on to the centre of a plate, hold it down and shake slightly. It should come out quite easily. Carefully flood the plate with the hot sauce and serve decorated with a small sprig of parsley.

Eggs Florentine

The name 'florentine' when attached to any savoury dish indicates that it is either based round or garnished with spinach. This is a delicious and simple dish, which makes an excellent starter for four or a light supper dish for two, yet few people seem to know how to make it. A true Eggs Florentine is made with soft-boiled, shelled eggs, although cheats rely on the eggs cooked in a poacher. Try the classic way first, it's very easy so long as you time it correctly.

Serves 2 or 4 (see above)
1½ lb (670 g) spinach
1 oz (30 g) butter
seasoning
pinch freshly grated nutmeg
4 eggs (size 2 or 3)

Sauce
1 oz (30 g) butter
1 tbsp unbleached plain flour
½ pint (300 ml) milk
2 oz (55 g) grated Parmesan
1 tsp Dijon mustard

Wash the spinach well in a sinkful of water and break off the stems. Put it into a pan with no added liquid and cook for 5 minutes, stirring occasionally, until tender and reduced in size. Drain and press between two plates to squeeze out all the surplus water. Return to the pan with 1 oz (30 g) butter, seasoning and some freshly grated nutmeg and set aside.

Bring a small pan of water to the boil and lower the eggs into it. (To prevent them from cracking, pierce one end with a fine needle – this allows the air in the egg to escape when it expands on heating.) Return rapidly to the boil and time to cook for 5 minutes from this point. Keep the cooking water and plunge the eggs into a bowl of cold water. Leave for 5-8 minutes while you make the cheese sauce.

Make a roux with the butter and flour and gradually add the milk, stirring until smooth. Mix in the cheese and mustard and cook for a few minutes. Leave over a very low heat.

To shell the eggs, which will be soft inside although the whites are hard, tap each one all over with a spoon until the shell is crazed. Remove a strip round the waist, using the handle of a metal teaspoon, and then gently pull off the remaining shell. Put the eggs back into their cooking water to heat through.

Reheat the spinach over a medium flame, tossing well, and divide into individual warmed gratin dishes. Arrange one hot whole egg on top of each (or two if you are serving this as a main course), coat with the sauce and sprinkle with a little more Parmesan. Quickly brown under a preheated grill and serve.

Spinach and Cream Cheese Lasagne

This vegetarian version of lasagne is absolutely delicious. If you can make it with ricotta, a soft white Italian cheese made from whey, this gives a lovely creamy texture, but low-fat cream cheese is a perfectly good substitute.

Serves 6
2¼-2½ lb (1-1.1 kg) fresh spinach
1 lb (450 g) ricotta or low-fat
   cream cheese
9 sheets lasagne

seasoning
1 portion all-purpose tomato
   sauce (see page 96)
3 oz (85 g) Cheddar cheese

First make the tomato sauce and simmer very gently with the lid on for 30 minutes. Check occasionally to make sure it isn't sticking.

   Wash and pick over the spinach and cook in a large pan with no extra water, turning occasionally until just tender. Drain, squeeze out all excess water and chop finely, then mix well with the cream cheese and some seasoning. Boil the lasagne in a large pan for about 7 minutes (fresh lasagne will take only about 30 seconds). Drain and immerse the sheets in a bowl of cold water until needed, to keep them separate.

   Grease an ovenproof dish about 7 x 9 inches (18 x 23cm) and layer up the various components in the following order : lasagne, spinach mixture, tomato sauce. Repeat, top with a final layer of lasagne and spread the surface with a little more tomato sauce. Sprinkle with grated Cheddar and bake uncovered in an oven preheated to Gas 6/400°F/200°C until the top is golden brown.

   This can be prepared in advance up to the final baking, but remember to remove the dish from the fridge in time to let it return to room temperature before putting it in the oven.

Strawberries

Wild strawberries are native to Europe and a cultivated descendant is the lovely *fraise de bois* or Alpine strawberry, sometimes found in Britain at good French or Italian restaurants, but always at a hefty price. The larger, juicier ones that we can get in such abundance during June and

July are the result of crossing, in the early nineteenth century, two varieties introduced to Europe from the eastern United States.

Whether they came from your garden or from a local pick-your-own farm, a good period of sunshine during ripening time can produce a veritable glut. Strawberries are highly perishable and cannot be stored, even in the fridge, for more than a day or two. Eat as many as you can fresh and make the rest into jam or purée to use as a base for mousses or ice-creams. Although out-of-season imported ones can be surprisingly good, others are disappointingly bland. A wet dull English summer also means rather tasteless strawberries which go squashy even more quickly than usual.

Don't wash strawberries unless absolutely necessary, as this increases the speed at which they deteriorate. If they are rather muddy or you suspect them of having come into contact with insecticides, wash them briefly under running water in a colander and use within hours. New methods of growing strawberries through holes pierced in sheets of black plastic stretched along the ground to keep down weeds and insects usually mean washing is not required.

When buying strawberries, go for the clear plastic punnets rather than the coloured or cardboard ones, as that way you can lift it up and see if any of the fruit are bad or squashed.

For other ways of serving strawberries as a dessert, see the recipes for Peaches and Strawberries Romanoff and Layered Fruit Pudding. You can also make a vinaigrette sauce with strawberries (see Avocado with Strawberry Sauce).

Chilled Strawberry Soup

This is prepared in a similar way to chilled cucumber soup, and makes an unusual start to a meal on a hot summer's day.

Serves 4

1 lb (450 g) strawberries
½ cucumber
2 small tubs (2 × 150 g) natural
  yoghurt

1 tbsp unrefined granulated
  sugar
1 tbsp fresh chopped mint
cold water
black pepper

Peel the cucumber and cut it into chunks. Hull the strawberries. Put everything except the water into a liquidizer and process until really smooth. Add enough cold water to bring the total volume to 1¾ pints (1 litre) amd process again. Pour into a soup tureen and chill for several hours.

Serve with a couple of fresh mint leaves floating in each bowl.

Strawberry and Cucumber Salad

It is always a good idea to try and bring a bit of variety and originality to a summer buffet, and this attractive and unusual salad fits the bill nicely, going particularly well with cold fish dishes like poached salmon. It certainly makes a change from the usual cucumber and chive salad, and is a good way to use up some of a bumper crop of strawberries.

Serves 6
12 oz (335 g) strawberries
1 medium-sized cucumber
black pepper

3 tbsp dry vermouth or white wine
2 tbsp finely snipped chives

Hull and halve the strawberries, after washing them briefly under cold running water if necessary. Peel the cucumber and slice it thinly, and arrange the slices round the outside of a round plate, followed by a ring of strawberry halves, and so on until you reach the centre of the dish. Season well with black pepper, pour over the vermouth or dry white wine and sprinkle with chopped chives. Chill until ready to serve.

Strawberry Crunch

The crunchy biscuit base of this dessert uses wholemeal digestive biscuits, made with organic flour, which you can find at wholefood and health shops. Use Greek cow's yoghurt for a creamier flavour.

Serves 8
1 lb (450 g) strawberries
9 oz (250 g) wholemeal digestive
   biscuits
3 oz (85 g) butter
2 tbsp lemon juice

2½ fl. oz (75ml) water
0.4 oz (11 g) sachet gelatine
2½ fl. oz (75 ml) whipping cream
5 oz (150 g) natural yoghurt
2 egg whites

Hull the strawberries and halve or quarter them, placing them in a bowl as you do so. Keep about 12 halves separate for decoration. Spread the biscuits out on a large board and crush well with a rolling pin. Melt the butter in a saucepan and add the crushed biscuits, stirring well to distribute the butter evenly. Empty into an 8 inch (20 cm) diameter cake tin with a removable bottom and press down well to form a base. Leave in the fridge to harden.

Put the lemon juice and water in a small saucepan and sprinkle the gelatine over them. When it has swollen and absorbed some of the liquid, heat very gently to dissolve. Add the strawberries and continue to heat gently, stirring, to draw out the strawberry juice, colouring the liquid a bright red. On no account let it boil, or the gelatine will form lumps. Leave to cool.

Before the strawberry mixture has had a chance to set, whip the cream and fold it in with the yoghurt. Don't worry if it looks a bit runny at this stage. Put into the fridge until on the point of setting, then whip the egg whites and fold them in. Pour on to the biscuit base and chill again until set.

Decorate with the reserved strawberries before serving.

Strawberry Yoghurt Ice-Cream

Strange as it may sound to traditionalists, yoghurt replaces cream very well in homemade ice-cream. Apart from being healthier it is of course much cheaper. Turning strawberries into ice-cream is an ideal way of using up ones that have passed peak condition and are beginning to go a bit mushy.

Serves 6

1¼ lb (550 g) strawberries	3 eggs
¼ pint (150 ml) water	8 oz (225 g) natural yoghurt

Wash the fruit briefly in a colander and shake dry. Put into a pan with the water and cook gently until really soft and juicy. Sieve into another saucepan.

Separate the eggs and put the yolks into a big bowl or food processor, then beat or process until light and smooth. Heat the sieved fruit until nearly boiling and pour it on to the egg yolks. If you are using a machine, do this with the engine running, if by hand wrap a twisted damp cloth tightly round the base of the bowl to hold it steady and beat while you pour. Add the yoghurt and beat until the whole mixture is smooth and well blended.

Tip into a fairly shallow dish or freezer box and freeze until it begins to turn firm and semi-frozen (this should take about an hour). Tip back into a bowl and beat till smooth (again you can use a food processor). Whip the egg whites until stiff, fold them in to the fruit mixture and refreeze.

Strawberries and Watermelon

English strawberries and imported watermelon appear on the market at about the same time and go together well in fruit salads, the soft sweetness of the berries contrasting with the crisp refreshing texture of the melon. Prepare this a couple of hours in advance to allow the cointreau to soak in, and put the ice-cream on top as you sit down to the first course, so it has time to melt slightly into the gaps in the mound of red fruit.

Serves 6
1 lb (450 g) strawberries
1 small watermelon (about 4 lb/
   1.8 kg)

4 tbsp cointreau
6 scoops strawberry yoghurt
   ice-cream (see above)

Halve the watermelon across its waist and run a knife round between the flesh and the shell. Cut the flesh into quarters, without piercing the skin, and carefully lift these out. Repeat with the other half. Slice the watermelon flesh into fairly large chunks – it is possible at this stage to remove most the pips if you want to, using a small coffee spoon.

Hull the strawberries and halve the larger ones. Fill the two watermelon shells with the strawberries and some of the melon, and place on a large platter, scattering the rest of the melon round the shells. Pour the cointreau over the fruit, cover with clingfilm and refrigerate.

Transfer the ice-cream from the freezer to the fridge about an hour before eating, so it is soft enough to scoop out. Before starting the meal, arrange some on the top of the filled melon shells. Garnish with fresh mint leaves. Depending on the weather and on how long you may be until you are ready for the dessert, you can either return the dish to the fridge or leave it out until serving.

HIGH SUMMER

Blackcurrants and Redcurrants

Blackcurrants, as well as their cousins the redcurrants (and the whitecurrants which are a variation of them), are fruit grown widely in Britain, Holland and other northern European countries, yet hardly heard of further south. As kitchen-garden enthusiasts are aware, the bushes yield heavy crops which require immediate picking when ripe or they will rot on the stalk, particularly in wet weather. It is sometimes quite a challenge to know how to deal with this abundance, but they can be converted not only into jams and jellies but also into delicious desserts, and can even be used as a stuffing for poultry.

The French grow blackcurrants primarily for converting into the alcoholic *crème de cassis*, which you mix with white wine to make Kir, a refreshing summer drink. The British have exploited blackcurrants' high vitamin C content and converted it into Ribena and other blackcurrant squash drinks, which incidentally are now free of artificial colour and available in low-sugar varieties.

Redcurrant jelly is of course a staple British accompaniment to lamb, and a good jam can be made when redcurrants are mixed with raspberries. Few people, however, have tried the many excellent desserts which can be made using red- and blackcurrants. These cost just a few pence if you grow your own, which is easy to do so long as you can keep the birds away (repairing and putting up the fruit cage netting is one of the most unpopular jobs in our family). Once established, the bushes crop heavily year after year.

Redcurrants are picked in small clusters, which look very pretty in fruit salads or as a garnish on desserts or plates of cheese. They are easy to strip off the stalk and therefore do not normally need to be sieved or strained. Blackcurrants, on the other hand, tend to come with a small stem or stalk still attached, as well as a woody little piece at the other end (once the flower head), both of which should, ideally be removed. The easiest way to do this is to cook them first and then sieve them, unless you are making a dish where they are needed whole, in which case you will have to pick off the stems one by one. Both black- and redcurrants freeze very well, and can be used straight from the freezer in most recipes calling for fresh ones with great success.

For a selection of recipes featuring redcurrants see page 83.

Blackcurrant and Fruit Compote

Use whatever fruits you can find in the shops or garden for this delicious hot fruit compote. If you make it in July, you should be able to combine all the fruits below. If you're eating it in August or September, try it with plums, blackberries and pears. Blackcurrants from your freezer can be used.

Serves 6

1 lb (450 g) blackcurrants
8 oz (225 g) dark cherries
8 oz (225 g) raspberries
2 peaches or nectarines or 6 apricots

2-3 tbsp clear honey
1 orange
2 tbsp brandy

Pick the stems off the blackcurrants, stone the cherries and pick over the raspberries. Halve the peaches or their substitute and stone them before slicing them. (Apricots should be left in halves.) Put the fruit into a saucepan with the honey, juice of the orange and the brandy and stir until the honey has dissolved and the fruit juices are beginning to run. Taste for sweetening and add more honey if necessary. Transfer to an uncovered ovenproof dish and put into an oven preheated to Gas 4/350°F/180°C for 20-30 minutes.

Serve with fromage frais or cream. On hot days chill the compote first.

Blackcurrant Yoghurt Mousse

This is a delicious mousse with a bright colour and refreshing flavour. I have used a tub of Greek cow's yoghurt instead of whipped double cream to cut down on the calories and fat. If you can't get this, use ordinary natural yoghurt, but as this is slightly sharper and less creamy than Greek, you may like to add a little extra sweetening.

I find it isn't necessary to use the whole packet of gelatine when making this mousse, try with about three-quarters of it instead.

Serves 4-6

8 oz (225 g) blackcurrants
3 tbsp clear honey
2 tbsp water
less than 0.4 oz (11 g) gelatine

8 oz (225 g) Greek or natural
   yoghurt
a little water
3 egg whites

Simmer the blackcurrants with the honey and a couple of tablespoons of water, stirring occasionally, until the fruit is really soft and the honey dissolved. Press through a sieve so you get a purée, then whisk in the yoghurt. Sprinkle the gelatine over 2-3 tablespoons of water in a small saucepan and leave to sponge. After a few minutes heat very gently so the gelatine dissolves. Stir this into the blackcurrant mixture and leave in the fridge until on the point of setting.

Whisk the egg whites until stiff and fold into the blackcurrants. Pour into a 1½ pint (850 ml) soufflé dish and leave to set for several hours.

Summer Pudding

This epitomizes English summers and the best of our national cooking. Easy to make, so long as you remember to do it the day before, it is always popular and, at the height of the soft fruit season, very cheap. Some recipes call for strawberries, but since these tend to ripen ahead of raspberries and currants, this isn't very practical. I feel you must include blackcurrants in order to get the wonderful purple juice, but whether you then add raspberries and redcurrants or just one of the two is up to you. Blackberries, too, can be used later in the season, and this pudding is very successful when made with frozen fruit.

If you are using only currants, you will need more honey to sweeten the dish than if you include raspberries. The bread should be a day old, so it is easier to mould into the basin.

Serves 6
1½-1¾ lb (670-785 g)   2-4 tbsp clear honey
   fruit (see above)   6 or more slices wholemeal bread

Wash the fruit in a colander and shake it dry. Put it into a saucepan with the honey and cook over a low heat, stirring occasionally, for 2-3 minutes until the juice begins to run and the honey is thoroughly dissolved. Don't overcook, though. Turn a 1½ pint (850 ml) pudding basin on to a piece of the bread and cut a circle round it. Line the basin with the remaining bread, removing the crusts first (it is easiest to fit the jigsaw if you cut the bread into triangular shapes). Pour in the cooled fruit with all the juice and top with the circular bread lid. Cover with a plate which fits inside the basin rim and weigh down with tins or heavy weights. Refrigerate overnight.

Shortly before serving, remove the weights and plate, cover with a shallow dish and up-end. Give a couple of sharp shakes side to side, holding the two dishes tightly together and then lift off the basin. If there are any patches where the juice has not fully stained the bread, just scoop some up from the 'moat' and pour over.

Serve, if you wish, with whipped cream, lightened by mixing in a stiffly whisked egg white.

Blackcurrant Suet Simmer

Suet puddings have gone out of favour recently, partly because of the move away from using rich animal fats. However, there is now a vegetable suet on the market which is just as good. This pudding is actually very quick to prepare, all you have to do during the cooking time is remember to check that the water isn't boiling dry. It is lighter than a traditional pudding, since the filling isn't encased in the suet pastry, just topped with it. This crust puffs up and absorbs some of the purple juice – which will also stain the cloth holding the pudding, so use an old one.

Serves 4

1 lb (450 g) blackcurrants
3-4 tbsp clear honey
a little water
Suet pastry
2 oz (55 g) wholemeal flour

2 oz (55 g) unbleached plain flour
2 level tsp baking powder
1 oz (30 g) shredded vegetable suet
2½ fl. oz (75 ml) water

Sift the flour into a large bowl, stir in the baking powder and suet. Using a normal table knife, mix in the water gradually until the dough has absorbed most of it, then turn out on to a lightly floured surface and knead gently until smooth. Leave to rest for 10-15 minutes.

Wash the blackcurrants if fresh and put them in a pan with the honey. If you are using frozen you may need a little water to start them cooking. Simmer gently until the juices begin to run freely and the honey has dissolved, then pour into a 1 pint (550 ml) pudding basin. Leave to cool a little.

Roll out the pastry and cut a circle slightly wider than the rim of the basin. Cover the basin with the pastry, cup your hands and put them round the rim, pressing the pastry against the china so it sticks. Trim off any surplus. Cover with a square of silver foil, pleated in the middle to allow room for the suet to puff up, and twist the edges to keep it in place. Then lay an old cloth or napkin over the foil, tie it into place round the rim with string, and bring the four corners up to tie into two knots for a handle. Lower into a pan containing simmering water that comes half-way up the side of the basin, put the lid on and leave to cook for 2 hours, topping up with more boiling water when necessary.

Serve with natural yoghurt or cream.

Blackcurrant Jelly

This makes a lovely rich jelly, very good on bread as well as a substitute for redcurrant jelly, served with lamb or poultry. You should remove any leaves but the stems can be left on.

3 lb (1.35 kg) blackcurrants   2¼ pints (1.3 litres) water
                                         unrefined granulated sugar

Wash the fruit in a colander under cold running water. Put it into a large pan with 1½ pints (850 ml) of the water and simmer until the fruit is soft and pulpy. Squash it against the side of the pan every so often with a big spoon. Leave to strain through a jelly bag into a large bowl for an hour. Return the fruit to the pan with the remaining ¾ pint (425 ml) water, simmer for 30 minutes and strain through the bag overnight.

    Measure the juice, pour it into a clean plan and mix with 1 lb (450 g) sugar to every pint (550 ml) of juice. Stir gently over a low heat until the sugar is completely dissolved, then boil rapidly until setting point is reached (see Jams and Jellies). Pour into warmed jars, cover and leave to grow cold in the usual way. Label and store in a cool, dry place.

Blackcurrant Jam

This jam is not often seen these days, but it has been a favourite of mine since childhood. Hours spent picking blackcurrants in the fruit cage at the top of the garden were a good excuse to avoid other less pleasurable household chores. The jam is quite chunky and is delicious with scones or thick slices of granary bread. Remove as much of the outer stems as possible, although the bit on the bottom of the berry is too small and fiddly to remove and can be left in – once cooked you don't notice it.

Makes about 5 lb (2.25 kg)
2 lb (900 g) blackcurrants   3 lb (1.35 kg) unrefined granulated
1½ pints (850 ml) water   sugar

Wash the currants in a colander under cold running water and put into a large pan with the water. Simmer until soft then stir in the sugar over a gentle heat until completely dissolved. Boil rapidly until setting point is reached (see Jams and Jellies). This jam sets easily since blackcurrants are high in pectin and acid. Pot and cover in the usual way, then leave to grow cold before labelling and storing in a cool dry place.

Cauliflower

Cauliflower first went on record as being grown in the Middle East and Cyprus, although it was supposed to have come originally from the East. It was probably introduced to Spain by the Arabs and worked its way north, arriving in Britain around the start of the eighteenth century.

The British climate is a little too severe to provide ideal growing conditions for cauliflowers. They cannot survive sharp frosts and disappear almost entirely (or become very expensive) during the months of December, January and Febuary. However in summer cauliflower is plentiful and cheap and, to my mind, much tastier too. This is the time to experiment with different recipes, and even to buy in bulk and use it to make piccalilli.

When buying a cauliflower you should examine its head closely, since some greengrocers cheat by shaving off any blackened or brown patches. The whole head should be firm, white and tightly curled, and the leaves round the base green and crisp. Any rank smell or flabbiness indicates it is well past its best. The individual little branches that fork out from the thick main stem are called florets. Foodies debate furiously whether a cauliflower should be boiled whole or cut into florets first. In fact you can do either, depending on which is more appropriate for your recipe, but if it is already broken up it will of course require less cooking time before it is tender.

Cauliflower will stay fresh in the bottom of the fridge for up to a week wrapped in a plastic bag but, like all vegetables, it is best eaten as freshly harvested as possible.

Cauliflower and Caraway Soup

Caraway seeds have a strong, distinctive taste which goes well with the unmistakable flavour of cauliflower. However, be careful not to add too many, or you will overwhelm the soup completely.

Serves 4

1 cauliflower	½ tsp caraway seeds
½ medium onion	1 pint (550 ml) chicken stock
small clove garlic	¾ pint (425 ml) milk
1 tbsp sunflower oil	black pepper
½ oz (15 g) butter	1-2 tbsp freshly chopped parsley

Trim the leaves from the cauliflower and cut into florets, removing most of the tough central stalk. Chop the onion. Heat the butter and oil in a saucepan and sauté the cauliflower with the crushed garlic and onion for about 5 minutes over a high heat, tossing frequently. Add the caraway seeds towards the end.

Pour in the chicken stock and simmer, covered, for 30 minutes. Liquidize together with the milk and pour back into the saucepan through a sieve to catch the seeds. Season with black pepper and a little salt if you feel it needs it, and serve sprinkled with chopped parsley.

Cauliflower Provençal

If you can't get fresh basil for this dish, substitute parsley instead. Dried basil is not really suitable as it has a rather bitter taste when cooked only briefly, nothing like the wonderful aromatic flavour of fresh basil leaves. This serves three to four as an accompanying vegetable or two as a simple supper dish.

Serves 2-4 (see above)

1 medium cauliflower
3 medium tomatoes
2 cloves garlic
2 tbsp olive oil

2-3 tbsp freshly chopped basil
black pepper
2 oz (55 g) mature Cheddar cheese

Divide the cauliflower into florets, blanch in boiling water for 4 minutes and drain. Skin the tomatoes, first dipping them into boiling water for 10 seconds and then into cold. Chop roughly. Sauté the garlic in the hot oil in a frying pan for a few seconds, then add the drained cauliflower and cook for a further 3 minutes, turning occasionally. Add the tomato and basil, lower the heat and cook for 5 minutes, covered.

Season with black pepper and sprinkle with the grated Cheddar. Toss the contents of the pan a little until the cheese melts and serve immediately.

Gorgonzola Cauliflower Cheese

Here is a really tasty alternative to the ubiquitous cauliflower cheese – made with gorgonzola. Any strong-tasting blue cheese can be substituted, but I find the ripe, full, gooey flavour of gorgonzola is particularly good.

Serves 2 as a main course, 4 as a side dish

1 cauliflower
½ pint (300 ml) milk
½ onion
bayleaf

4 oz (110 g) gorgonzola cheese
¾ oz (20 g) butter
¾ oz (20 g) unbleached plain flour
2-3 tbsp wholemeal breadcrumbs

Trim the leaves and thick base stalk from the cauliflower, but keep it whole. Bring a pan of water to the boil, drop the cauliflower head in, stalk down, and simmer for 15 minutes. Meanwhile bring the milk to the boil in a small pan with the sliced onion and bayleaf, remove immediately from the heat and leave to infuse so that it absorbs the flavours. Grate the cheese.

Preheat the oven to Gas 6/400°F/200°C. Strain the flavoured milk into a jug, make a roux with the butter and flour and stir in the milk until you have a smooth sauce. Simmer very gently for about 5 minutes before stirring in the grated cheese.

Drain the cauliflower well, making sure you get rid of all the water trapped inside it, or it will spoil the sauce. Put in the centre of a shallow ovenproof dish and pour the sauce all over it. Sprinkle with the breadcrumbs and put into the oven until browned (about 10-15 minutes).

Cauliflower Polonaise

When simply cooked (though not overdone), cauliflower is an excellent accompaniment to almost all fish and meat dishes. It does lack a certain something visually, though, not being the most colourful of vegetables. Serve it with this garnish to liven up the plate.

Serves 4

1 cauliflower	2 oz (55 g) butter
2 eggs	2 tbsp fresh chopped parsley
2 oz (55 g) dried	black pepper
wholemeal breadcrumbs	squeeze lemon juice

Trim any leaf off the cauliflower and cook it whole in boiling water for 10-15 minutes until just tender – don't overdo it. Hardboil the eggs. Drain the cauliflower and keep it warm while you shell the eggs. Remove the yolks to a sieve and chop the whites finely.

Fry the breadcrumbs until browned in the butter. Divide the cauliflower into florets and arrange them on a circular dish with the stalks pointing inwards. Put the egg whites and parsley in the centre, sieve the yolks over the cauliflower itself, season with a few grinds of black pepper and a squeeze of lemon juice, and scatter with the breadcrumbs before serving.

Curried Cauliflower

For those who love curries, here is a terrific way of serving this strong-tasting vegetable, either as a side dish or as a meal in itself. I prefer to use the different spices for a finer flavour, but curry powder would do.

Serves 4

1 medium-large cauliflower
1 medium onion
2 cloves garlic
3 tbsp sunflower oil
1 tsp cumin seeds
3 tsp ground turmeric

½ tsp chilli powder
3-4 medium tomatoes
¾ pint (425 ml) water
1 oz (30 g) split
   blanched almonds
2 tsp cornflour

Cut the large base off the cauliflower and discard it with the leaves. Split the head into its natural branches, so that you end up with quite large florets. Slice the onion and cook it in the oil in a heavy-bottomed flameproof casserole or saucepan with the crushed garlic and spices for a little more than 5 minutes, over a fairly low heat. Meanwhile peel the tomatoes by dipping them in boiling water for 10 seconds and then into cold to loosen the skins.

Chop the tomatoes roughly, add them to the spices and cook for a further 5 minutes. Add the water and the cauliflower florets, bring to the boil, cover and simmer for 10 minutes. Brown the almonds on an oiled baking sheet in a hot oven, but don't let them burn. Test to see if the cauliflower is tender and lift it out on to a serving dish. Mix the cornflour with a tablespoon or two of cold water, stir it into the sauce and return to the boil. As soon as it thickens, pour the sauce over the cauliflower and sprinkle with the almonds.

Piccalilli

This is one of the many chutneys and pickles which Britain's colonial days in India introduced to our storecupboards and is an excellent way of using up a surplus of vegetables at the end of the summer. It is not for the fainthearted ! The vegetables can be varied, but should include cauliflower, onions and something green like beans, marrow or green tomatoes.

Makes about 6 lb (2.75 kg)

2-3 cauliflowers (about 2 lb or
   900 g) weighed after trimming
1 lb (450 g) French beans
1 lb (450 g) pickling onions
salt
5 chillies
1 oz (30 g) fresh ginger

2 pints (1.1 litres) white wine
   vinegar
1 oz (30 g) wholemeal flour
½ oz (15 g) turmeric
2 oz (55 g) English mustard powder
1 oz (30 g) celery seeds
4 oz (110 g) light muscovado sugar
   (optional)

Cut the cauliflower into small florets. Top and tail the beans and slice,

peel and halve or quarter the pickling onions depending on size. Put all
the vegetables into a large bowl and sprinkle well with salt. Leave for
18-24 hours.

The next day, rinse off the salt and drain well. Halve and deseed the
chillies (wearing rubber gloves to protect your hands) and finely chop
the ginger. Put the vegetables in a large pan with the vinegar, chillies
and chopped ginger, bring to the boil and simmer for 5 minutes.
Strain, reserving the vinegar. Mix the flour with the other spices and
gradually blend in the vinegar. Simmer for about 10-15 minutes until it
has thickened, while you pack the vegetables into warm jars. Pour the
thickened vinegar over these until they are completely covered and seal.

You can make a sweeter version of this by adding a little sugar when
you return the vinegar to the pan for thickening.

Courgettes

Courgettes belong to the gourd family, which includes pumpkins, squash
and – more distantly – cucumbers and melons. Courgettes are really
miniature marrows, bred specially to be harvested while small, rather
than growing into the large, watery marrow once so much a part of the
worst of British cooking. If you grow your own you will find that they
come on in a rush and you need to pick them daily to avoid ending up
with oversize courgettes. At the end of the summer in particular they are
very plentiful, and extremely cheap to buy too.

In Britain courgettes were until recently a luxury vegetable, and for
this reason most of us have only a small repertoire of different ways to
cook them. This becomes stretched to the limit in high season, which is
the time to experiment with a wider range of recipes. Courgettes are
quick and easy to prepare, needing only to be wiped with a damp cloth
before using. Choose ones that are firm and glossy-skinned – those
showing signs of flabbiness or softness should be avoided. In America
they are called zucchini, a word introduced with the Italian immigrants.

All courgettes have a high water content and do not benefit from
being plainly boiled. Lightly sautéing them in a little butter brings out
the best in them, but if you want to keep your fat intake low, toss them in
a very little water or stock. Small ones can be sliced or grated to be eaten
raw in salads, and they are a good ingredient in stir-fry vegetable dishes,
since they need so little cooking.

For other ways of using a surplus of courgettes, see Ratatouille and
Tomato Chutney.

Courgettes Stuffed with Minced Lamb

Most of the Mediterranean and Middle Eastern cuisines have stuffed vegetables as a standard dish, be it aubergines, mushrooms, big beef tomatoes or, as here, courgettes. I like the stuffing to be full of flavour without being fussy, and I prefer to be able to identify each taste. This isn't possible if the whole dish is drowned in a thick cheese sauce, which is how stuffed courgettes are often served in England. Here is my adaptation of the Middle Eastern style of stuffing, featuring that region's staples of lamb and mint.

This serves four as a first course, but is quite filling. Increase the ingredients by half and you could serve it as a main dish (allowing three courgette halves per person). Choose fair-sized, plump courgettes, keeping the tiny ones for eating as a plain vegetable or in a salad.

Serves 4 as a starter

4 courgettes
8 oz (225 g) lamb fillet
1 medium onion
1 large clove garlic
2 tbsp olive oil
seasoning

1 tsp fennel seeds
1 tsp ground coriander
2 tbsp fresh chopped mint
2 small tomatoes
1 portion all-purpose
    tomato sauce (see page 96)

First make the tomato sauce and leave it to simmer gently, stirring occasionally, for 20 minutes.

Wipe the courgettes, top and tail them and cut them in half lengthways. Using a sharp knife or teaspoon scoop out a funnel down the centre of each half, to create a container for the stuffing. Set the flesh to one side. Simmer the courgettes in a little unsalted water for 5 minutes, then carefully lift out each one with a slotted spoon. If they break, don't worry, reassemble them when you add the stuffing and no one will be any the wiser.

Mince the lamb or chop it finely in a food processor. Finely chop the onion and mix it with the lamb, then sauté lightly in the oil with the crushed garlic until browned. Add the seasoning, fennel seeds, coriander and mint. Finely chop the scooped-out courgette flesh, cut the tomatoes into small dice and add these to the mixture. Cook briskly until the excess water has evaporated – about 10 minutes. Pile the mixture down the centre of the courgettes, pressing it in well. Pour the tomato sauce into a shallow ovenproof dish, arrange the courgette halves, filling uppermost, on top and bake in an oven preheated to Gas 5/375°F/190°C for 30-40 minutes.

Courgette Soufflé

At the mention of soufflé, most people think of ones made with cheese, ham or spinach. Courgettes too make a delightful soufflé, flecked with green and very light. This is best served as a starter, or a lunch dish for two, as it is not very filling.

Serves 4 as a starter

8 oz (225 g) courgettes
1½ oz (45 g) butter
½ pint (300 ml) milk
½ onion
bayleaf
black peppercorns

1 oz (30 g) unbleached plain flour
seasoning
2 oz (55 g) Cheddar or Cheshire
  cheese
3 eggs

Top and tail the courgettes and grate them. Heat a small knob (about ½ oz/15 g) of the butter in a saucepan and cook the courgettes in it for a few minutes until much of the water has been extracted from them. Drain, dry and set aside. If you omit this step the bottom of the soufflé will be very wet, as courgettes have a high water content.

Heat the milk together with the peeled half onion, bayleaf and black peppercorns. When it comes to the boil, remove from the heat and set aside to infuse for 5 minutes before straining into a jug. Melt the rest of the butter in a non-stick pan, stir in the flour and make a light roux. Blend in the flavoured milk until you have a smooth béchamel sauce, season, then leave it to simmer gently for 5-10 minutes while you grate the cheese and separate the eggs.

Remove the pan from the heat, cool slightly and stir the cheese and beaten egg yolks into the béchamel with the grated courgettes. Whip the eggs whites stiffly, fold them into the courgette mixture and pour into a buttered 2 pint (1.1 litre) soufflé dish. Cook in an oven preheated to Gas 6/400°F/200°C for 25-30 minutes until well risen and firm to the touch. Serve immediately.

Courgette and Carrot Salad

I have called this a salad, but as an alternative to eating it raw you can equally well sauté the vegetables lightly in butter and drain off any excess water before serving hot. It is extremely quick to prepare if you have a food processor with a grater blade.

Serves 4

2-3 medium sized courgettes
3 medium carrots

¼ medium green pepper
1 tbsp roasted sesame seeds
French dressing (see page 181)

Top and tail the courgettes and grate them. Peel the carrots and do likewise. Slice the green pepper quarter, cutting out any soft white core or pips. Drain off any excess water from the courgettes before mixing everything together along with the sesame seeds and French dressing.

Courgette Fritters

In my view courgettes are the best vegetables to make into fritters and I have tasted some really good examples at even the most ordinary Italian restaurants. If you grow your own courgettes, you may enclose the plant's flower in batter too and eat that. Make sure you wash it first though, and dry lightly. Choose courgettes that aren't too small, or you'll be eating all batter and little vegetable. Serve as a starter or to accompany a simple main course like grilled fish or veal escalopes.

Serves 4
4-6 medium courgettes

Batter
4 oz (110 g) unbleached plain flour
pinch salt
1 tbsp sunflower oil

¼ pint (150 ml) water
1 egg white
sunflower oil for frying

Sieve the flour into a bowl with the salt. With your hand make a slight well in the centre and pour in the oil and the water gradually, stirring steadily to draw in the flour from round the edge. Beat until smooth (you can do this with an electric whisk) and leave to rest for 30 minutes to an hour.

Top and tail the courgettes and then slice them fairly thickly at a diagonal angle, about 45°. You will end up with quite long slanting slices. Whisk the egg white until stiff and fold it into the fritter batter. Coat the courgette slices and immediately shallow or deep fry in really hot oil until crisp. If you want to keep some warm while cooking the remainder, put them in a low oven but do not cover the dish or the batter will go soggy.

Courgette-Stuffed Trout

This light, easy to prepare and unusual stuffing for trout makes a healthily low-fat dish.

Serves 4
3 medium courgettes
4 trout, gutted
4 tsp fromage frais or low-fat
   cream cheese

pinch thyme
seasoning
2 tbsp fresh orange juice

Wash the trout well, particularly on the inside, where you should run
your fingernail along any places where blood is still trapped near the
backbone. Wipe the courgettes, top, tail and then grate them. Mix with
the fromage frais, thyme, seasoning and a good squeeze of orange
juice before filling the belly cavities of the trout. Wrap each fish in a
parcel of lightly oiled silver foil and bake in an oven preheated to
Gas 6/400°F/200°C for 20 minutes until the fish is white when scraped at
the shoulder.

Cucumbers

These days everybody expects to eat identical salads all the year round
and seems to be prepared to pay amazing sums for cucumbers in winter.
Essentially, though, cucumber is a summer vegetable, at its best,
cheapest and most plentiful during the months when it ripens quickly
and naturally under even a feeble British summer sun.

Cucumber keeps quite well in the fridge, but since it is 90 per cent
water (and therefore, incidentally, very low in calories) it is unsuitable
for freezing and it is sometimes hard to know how, for example, to use up
the rest of the large plump cucumber you bought for a small salad earlier
in the week. As well as being popular raw, however, it combines well
with a variety of other summer produce and responds also to gentle
braising or sautéing, especially if you add fresh herbs.

Cucumbers have been grown for eating for several thousand years,
particularly in the Far and Middle East, but only became popular here in
the seventeenth century. Different countries grow and favour different
varieties, those seen most commonly in Britain being the long, smooth-
skinned type grown in greenhouses, which have a mild, refreshing taste.
However, it is also worth trying the shorter stubbier ones sold in shops
used by a Middle Eastern clientele, which should be peeled and sampled
for bitterness before using. Home-grown varieties are less often bitter
than they used to be, now that milder strains have been developed.

If the skin does look a bit tough, which can be the case with older
cucumbers, try to pare off just the very outer layer with a potato peeler,
leaving the bright green flesh immediately underneath. Or you can
remove the skin in alternate strips, which looks attractive as well as
leaving some of the distinctive taste behind.

For excellent summer salads using cucumber see also Mint and Cucumber
Yoghurt Salad, and Strawberry and Cucumber Salad. For other uses see
the recipes for Chilled Strawberry Soup and Andalusian Gazpacho, and
for the Watercress Sauce to accompany Hot Poached Salmon.

Cucumber Canapés

Don't forget that cucumber provides an excellent base for canapés, so long as you don't prepare it too far in advance, in which case the juice tends to leak out. It is also good cut into batons as part of a selection of crudités surrounding a bowl of dip – something which always gets eaten up at a drinks party.

Makes about 20 canapés

1 thin-skinned cucumber
8 oz (225 g) of one of the following
taramasalata
cream cheese mixed with garlic
  and chopped fresh herbs

crabmeat mixed with a
  little stiff mayonnaise
kipper or smoked mackerel pâté

chopped parsley
stuffed olives

With a potato peeler remove the skin from the cucumber in alternate strips, so some remains to provide an attractive visual effect. Then slice the whole length into rounds about ¼-½ inch (0.5-1.25 cm) thick. Using a piping bag and nozzle, squeeze a little of one of the spreads on top of each slice, in a swirl. The ones above combine well with the flavour and crispness of cucumber, although you could try others. Garnish with a little chopped parsley or a slice of stuffed green olive.

Alternatively slice the cucumber in half along its length and scoop out the seeds. Cut off a thin strip all the way along the bottom of each half so the wedges will sit flat on a plate. Using a piping bag and starred nozzle, pipe a thick strip of any of the above pâtés all the way along the scooped-out depression. Sprinkle with chopped parsley and, shortly before serving, cut the cucumber halves across into 1 inch (2.5 cm) lengths.

Cold Cucumber Soup

Cool, refreshing and light – in fact everything that summer food should be – this is a soup that takes very little time to prepare. A liquidizer is essential and means the preparation takes seconds.

Serves 4

1 large cucumber
1 tbsp wine vinegar
1 dsp cider vinegar
1-1½ tbsp fresh chopped mint

¾ pint (425 ml) natural yoghurt
2½ fl. oz (75 ml) single cream
½ tsp salt
black pepper

Wash the cucumber. If you think the skin is likely to be bitter (some home-grown varieties sometimes are) you should peel it, but the hothouse sort you find in the shops has a mild-tasting skin. Cut the cucumber into chunks and put it in a liquidizer with all the other

ingredients. Process until smooth and and refrigerate until ready to serve.
Garnish each bowl with the tip of a sprig of mint.

Hot Cucumber Soup with Watercress

Here is a very tasty soup, which is totally different from the chilled one
above. It is thickened with potato and flecked green with chopped
watercress.

Serves 4

1½ cucumbers
½ medium onion
1 oz (30 g) butter
8 oz (225 g) potatoes
¾ pint (425 ml) chicken stock

bayleaf
½ pint (300 ml) milk
black pepper
½ bunch watercress

Slice the onion and soften it in the butter in a saucepan. Peel and dice
the potatoes. Cut the cucumbers into chunks and add with the potato to
the pan. Pour in the chicken stock and add the bayleaf, bring to the boil
and simmer, covered, for 30 minutes. Cool slightly, liquidize and return
to the pan with the milk. Season with a little pepper.

Wash the watercress and cut off the stalks, then chop it very finely
before adding to the soup. Return to a simmer before serving.

Hot Cucumber with Dill

Many people do not think of cooking cucumber, tending to see it
exclusively as a salad vegetable. It is, however, a good way to use home-
grown cucumbers that turn out to be rather bitter, since in cooking the
taste becomes more mellow. This dish has a refreshing flavour that goes
well with curries and other spicy food.

Serves 4

1½ cucumbers
½ oz (15g) butter

1 tbsp freshly chopped dill
   or 1 tsp dried

Cut the ends off the cucumbers and then quarter lengthways. Slice the
quarters across into 1 inch (2.5 cm) pieces and cook them in the butter
in a covered saucepan for about 10 minutes until tender. Shake the pan
frequently to ensure even cooking, then sprinkle with fresh dill and
serve.

If you cannot find fresh dill, dried will do, but you should add it before you start to sauté the cucumbers.

Cooked Cucumber Salad

In South East Asia it is common to cook vegetables with spices before cooling them and serving as a salad. This cucumber version would go well with a cold fish dish in summer, or a Chinese-style main course like the recipe for Peking Turkey. Try to use sesame oil if you can, it adds an authentic Eastern flavour, although sunflower would do as a last resort. Sesame oil is stocked by Chinese supermarkets and quite a few wholefood shops.

Serves 4-6

1 cucumber
1 dsp salt
4 spring onions
1 tbsp sesame oil

good pinch chilli powder
2 tbsp soy sauce
1 tsp unrefined granulated sugar
1 tbsp roasted sesame seeds

Cut the cucumber into thin matchsticks about 2 inches (5 cm) long. Put these in a colander, sprinkle with the salt and leave for half an hour, then squeeze in your hands, rinse well and pat dry in absorbent kitchen paper. Finely chop three of the spring onions and fry them with the cucumber in the hot oil in a wok or frying pan for 2 minutes or so. Stir in the chilli and cook a further minute, then mix in the soy sauce, sugar and sesame seeds. Transfer to a dish and leave for a couple of hours.

Just before serving, chop the remaining onion and sprinkle it over the cucumber.

Cooked Stuffed Cucumber

When cooked the taste of cucumber alters subtly and blends in well with other cooked vegetables. This way of stuffing it makes an excellent starter or vegetarian main course.

Serves 4 as a starter, 2 as a main course

1 large cucumber
2 oz (55 g) brown rice
½ medium onion
small clove garlic
1 oz (30 g) butter
4 oz (110 g) mushrooms

pinch dried basil
1 medium tomato
½ tsp tomato purée
1 tbsp fresh chopped parsley
seasoning

Put the rice on to cook. This will take between 25 and 45 minutes depending on whether you have the easy-cook variety or normal brown rice. Cut the very end pieces off the cucumber, then halve it lengthways and across, so you have 4 pieces. Scoop out the seeds with a teaspoon and drop the cucumber pieces into boiling water to simmer gently for 15 minutes until tender.

Meanwhile prepare the filling. Chop the onion and sweat it in the butter with the crushed garlic for 5 minutes. Chop the mushrooms and add them with the basil, chopped tomato and tomato purée. Cook gently until the mushrooms are soft. If the cucumbers are ready before this, drain them and keep them warm.

Drain the rice and mix it into the mushroom filling with the parsley, seasoning well. Fill the centres of the cucumbers and serve immediately.

Cucumber Sauce

When you are preparing a special buffet with a salmon or salmon trout as a centrepiece, this is a delicious sauce to serve with it. If you prefer to keep your fat levels lower, substitute more yoghurt for the cream, but note that this will give a sharper flavour. Try and use Greek cow's yoghurt, which has a creamier taste. Margarine is not a suitable alternative for butter in this recipe.

Serves 6-8

1 cucumber
4 egg yolks
5 oz (140 g) butter
4 tbsp dry white wine
2 tbsp wine vinegar

seasoning
¼ pint (150 ml) whipping cream
¼ pint (150 ml) natural yoghurt
1 tsp lemon juice

Put the egg yolks in a pudding basin over a pan half filled with simmering water. Cut the butter into small pieces and add them gradually, as if making a hollandaise sauce. Stir all the time as the butter melts. Add the wine, vinegar and seasoning and continue stirring while the sauce thickens, then remove from the heat.

Peel and deseed the cucumber and whizz it up briefly in a liquidizer, but be careful not to reduce it to a liquid. Lightly whip the cream and mix it with the yoghurt and lemon juice and stir into the sauce with the cucumber. Serve at room temperature.

French Beans

Although best when home-grown and eaten within a few hours of picking, French beans (unlike broad beans or peas) perish less quickly between farm and market. Thus those in the shops are of a high standard and in summer fall in price to a level where you can buy them often and enjoy them served in many different ways.

Otherwise known as haricot or green beans, they originated in central America, and indeed are still flown in from Guatemala to be sold in Britain during the winter (at vast prices). It is the Aztec word, *ayecotl*, which gives them their name, corrupted to 'haricot'. The French call the fresh whole beans *haricots verts*, but we tend to use the term French beans since it was from France that they were first introduced to Britain on any scale. When small they are eaten whole. Much larger ones are shelled and the beans inside either dried to become what we call haricot beans, or eaten fresh, which is rare in England.

Apart from a brief wash under running water, French beans just need to be topped and tailed, although larger ones may need the string on the side pulled off too. When freshly cooked in water (which takes 10 minutes or less) they should be bright green – khaki-coloured ones are overdone and will have lost both flavour and texture.

A glut in the garden provides an opportunity not only to make a variety of delicious dishes, but to freeze some for the winter. Even city dwellers should buy up a large box or two of low-price beans in the summer for eating later, since they survive the freezer very well and come out much tastier and less watery than the commercially frozen varieties.

French Bean Soup

A simple tasty soup. Be careful not to overcook the beans, or you will lose the bright colour as well as the fresh flavour.

Serves 4

12 oz (335 g) French beans	1½ pints (850 ml) chicken stock
1 medium onion	1 tbsp fresh chopped parsley
1 clove garlic	seasoning
1 oz (30 g) butter	2-3 tbsp single cream

Top and tail the beans and cut them into ¼ inch (½ cm) pieces. Chop the onion and cook it very gently in the butter with the crushed garlic with the lid on, until soft (about 5 minutes). Add the beans and the stock and bring to the boil. Simmer for about 6-7 minutes until the beans are just tender. Liquidize the soup with the parsley and taste for seasoning – it is worth adding a fair amount of black pepper. Stir in the cream and reheat before serving with thick slices of wholemeal bread.

French Beans Mimosa

Cold French beans, in a salad, are just as good as hot ones. Here they are combined with another good summer vegetable, mangetout, the tiny variety of pea where you eat the whole pod as well. Do not pour the dressing on until shortly before serving, or the beans will go a less attractive khaki colour. The name derives from the sieved egg yolk, which resembles a flowering mimosa.

Serves 4

12 oz (335 g) French beans
4 oz (110 g) mangetout
1 egg (size 1 or 2)

French dressing made with
lemon juice instead of vinegar
(see page 181)

Top and tail the beans. Do the same with the mangetout, pulling off any stringy thread down the side of the larger ones. Drop the beans into a pan of slightly salted boiling water and simmer for 5 minutes. Add the mangetout, return to the boil and simmer another 2 minutes. Test to see if they are ready, then drain and run under cold water.

Hardboil the egg and shell it. Cut it in half, remove the yolk and chop the white with a stainless steel knife. Make the French dressing. Arrange the beans in a circular bowl, pointing inwards, with the mangetout inserted in between.

Just before serving, pour the French dressing over the salad, pile the chopped white in the centre and sieve the yolk in a wider circle round it.

French Beans Provençal

Instead of simply boiling them and serving plain, try serving French beans like this as an accompanying vegetable, which is particularly good with a roast or with grilled fish or steak.

Serves 4

12 oz (335 g) French beans

Sauce
½ medium onion
1 clove garlic
1 tbsp olive oil

1 lb (450 g) ripe tomatoes
  or 14 oz (390 g) tin
1 tbsp fresh basil or
  1 tsp dried
black pepper
bayleaf
2 oz (55 g) stoned green olives

Top and tail the beans and cut them in half. If you are using fresh tomatoes, peel them by dipping into boiling water for 10 seconds and then into cold to loosen the skins, then chop roughly. Chop the onion and sauté it in the oil with the garlic in a medium-sized saucepan or flameproof casserole for 5 minutes. Add the tomatoes, basil, black pepper and bayleaf and simmer for 10 minutes. Halve the olives.

Remove the bayleaf and liquidize the sauce briefly. Then return it to the pan with the olives and the beans, and simmer gently, stirring occasionally, for 10 minutes or so until the beans are tender.

Stir-Fried French Beans with Mangetout

Here is another dish using mangetout with French beans. You can of course serve the beans alone if you wish, but I rather like the Chinese way of mixing different colours and textures in a quick stir-fried dish.

Serves 4
12 oz (335 g) French beans
8 oz (225 g) mangetout
1 small red pepper
2-3 tbsp sunflower oil
1 clove garlic

up to ¼ pint (150 ml) chicken
  stock
1 tbsp soy sauce
1 dsp dry sherry
black pepper

Top and tail the beans and cut them into two or three pieces, depending on size. Cut the stalk end off the mangetout and pull off any tough stringy bits at the side. Halve the red pepper, deseed it and slice finely.

Heat the oil in a wok or large sauté pan and add the beans. Fry over a high heat, tossing and turning with a spoon or chopstick for 3 minutes. Add the crushed garlic, mangetout and red pepper and sauté a further minute or two. Pour in the stock – enough to nearly cover but not drown the vegetables. Bring to the boil and simmer for 1 minute, then add the soy sauce and sherry. Season well and serve.

The vegetables should still be a little crunchy.

French Beans in Almond Sauce

This is a low-fat way of serving beans with a lovely creamy sauce, using natural yoghurt instead of cream. By adding the cornflour you help prevent the yoghurt curdling. If you can find Greek cow's yoghurt, it has a creamier, richer flavour and texture. This would go well with a simply cooked fish like trout.

Serves 4
1 lb (450 g) French beans
4 spring onions
½ oz (15 g) butter
2 tbsp sunflower oil
4 oz (110 g) ground almonds
1 level tsp ground cinnamon

small carton (150 g)
  natural yoghurt
½ tsp cornflour
1 tbsp cold water
seasoning

Top and tail the beans and cut them in half. Trim the spring onions and
slice them, not too thinly. Heat the butter and oil in a thick-bottomed
saucepan or frying pan and stir-fry the vegetables for about 7 minutes,
until tender. Mix the almonds and cinnamon with the yoghurt. Dissolve
the cornflour in the tablespoon of cold water and beat into the yoghurt.
Pour this over the beans, season lightly and heat through until it just
reaches simmering point before serving.

Peaches

Peaches have until recently always been associated with luxury. The rich
impale them with a silver fork, before delicately pulling off the skin with
a small knife and slicing the fruit into slivers. (Presumably this originated
from the days when ladies wore long evening gloves at dinner.) Painters
have extolled them, women's skin has been compared to them and
cosmetic companies have slapped them on the label of every possible
product in an effort to imply that it will give your complexion a feeling of
natural smoothness and health.

Once available only at high prices, peaches now sell in season for next
to nothing. This is the time when you want to think of other ways to
serve them than with the traditional silver fork! Take advantage of their
cheapness to make the most of them while fresh as well as to preserve
them for the winter.

The peach originally arrived in Europe from China via Persia, and
apart from a few large country houses that had the labour to spare to tend
to a couple of peach trees grown against a south-facing wall, they have
always been imported. There are white and golden varieties, the first
being superior in flavour, but much rarer. Recently nectarines have
become increasingly popular. These are smooth-skinned without the
down which grows on the outside of peaches, and have a very good,
slightly richer flavour.

Peaches are one of the few fresh fruits that I tend to buy in a
supermarket, since most greengrocers in this country will not allow you
to pick them up. A ripe peach should be slightly soft all over, with a
smooth unwrinkled skin and a pale creamy-golden colour underneath
any red blush – if the base colour is too pale or has touches of green, it is
underripe. (This should not be confused with the less common white
variety.) However long you keep underripe peaches or nectarines or
however soft they become, the full sweet flavour will never develop.
Bought ready to eat they can be stored in the fridge for up to a fortnight.

Nectarines and peaches can be used more or less interchangeably in
many recipes, although they do taste slightly different. The advantage of

nectarines is that their peel is much more pleasant to eat than that of a peach. A quick way of peeling a peach is to dip it briefly in boiling water and then into cold, after which the skin should slip off quite easily.

Gammon with Peaches

Gammon is a lovely dish, hot or cold. If serving it hot, add skinned peaches for the last fifteen minutes of baking and serve with the hot peach sauce below. The sauce goes equally well cold with leftover sliced gammon. A joint of boiling bacon makes a cheaper, surprisingly good, substitute.

Serves 6

3 lb (1.35 kg) gammon
3 peaches
1 onion
cloves
parsley stalks
bayleaf
2 carrots
2 tbsp dark muscovado sugar
1 dsp wine vinegar

3 level tsp French mustard
1 tbsp clear honey

Sauce
6 peaches
pinch cinnamon
grated nutmeg
few blades mace
2 tsp dark muscovado sugar

Soak the gammon overnight in a pan of cold water to remove any saltiness. The next day, drain it, return it to the pan, cover with cold water and add the onion stuck with a few cloves, parsley stalks, bayleaf and quartered carrots. Bring to the boil, skim well to remove the scum and simmer for about 20 minutes to the 1lb (450 g) weight, minus about 15 minutes.

After this time remove from the stock (which you may use for bean and ham soup if it's not too salty), and cut off the outer skin of the gammon. Score the white fat underneath in a lattice pattern and stud each square with a clove. Mix the sugar, vinegar, mustard and honey together and spoon over the outside of the gammon. Bake in a shallow dish or tin which is not much bigger than the joint, in an oven preheated to Gas 4/350°F/180°C for 30 minutes, basting frequently. Peel the 3 peaches by briefly dipping them in boiling water then in cold to loosen the skins, cut in half and twist gently to remove the stones, and add to the gammon for the last 15 minutes of baking.

Meanwhile make the sauce. Skin, halve and chop the 6 peaches. Cook them gently in a small saucepan with the spices and sugar for 10 minutes, then liquidize or rub through a sieve. Serve separately in a warmed sauceboat.

Peaches and Strawberries Romanoff

Two priorities I always keep in mind when deciding which summer desserts to serve are appearance and speed of preparation. No one wants to spend hours fiddling around in the kitchen when everyone else is sitting in the garden enjoying the rare appearance of the sun, yet you don't want your food to look slapdash and unappetizing. Fruit and things like sorbets always look attractive served in a glass bowl (or individual glass bowls if you have them). This dessert can be prepared some way in advance and left in the fridge to absorb the flavours – it is also very quick to make. Use any orange liqueur such as Cointreau, Grand Marnier or Orange Curaçao.

Serves 4

4 peaches plus 2 very ripe ones   3 tbsp orange-flavoured liqueur
8-12 oz (225-335 g) strawberries

Skin all the peaches and halve them, removing the stone. Slice 4 and put them in a glass bowl. Put the remaining 2 in a liquidizer or food processor with a tablespoon or two of water and reduce to a purée. Hull and halve the strawberries and add them to the glass bowl. Pour on the liqueur and strain the peach juice on through a sieve. Leave in the fridge to absorb the flavours for at least an hour before serving.

If you wish, you may serve this with Chantilly cream (whipped cream flavoured with a few drops of vanilla essence).

Peaches in Fresh Fruit Jelly

If you have a ring mould, use it for this recipe to create a really attractive end-result, otherwise a soufflé dish will do. This makes an ideal dessert for a summer lunch or dinner party.

Serves 6

4 peaches   around ¾ pint (425 ml) water
1 lemon   1½ x 0.4 oz (11 g) sachets
2 oranges   powdered gelatine

Peel the peaches in the usual way, halve them and remove the stone. Slice each half thinly and lay the slices round a ring mould or in a dish, with the rounded side on the outside of the circle. Continue layering up until all the peaches have been used. Squeeze the juice from the lemon and oranges and make up to a pint with water in a saucepan. Sprinkle the gelatine over the surface and then heat the liquid gently, without stirring, until the gelatine has completely dissolved. Stir well then pour carefully over the peaches. Cool and leave in the fridge for about 3 hours to set.

To serve, ease round the edge of the jelly with a sharp knife. Dip the base of the mould briefly in very hot water, then up-end it on to a plate and shake slightly. It should slip out quite easily.

Peach Flan

Here is a perfect example of baking a pastry case blind before filling it with the fruit. You can serve this cold or straight after grilling the top of it.

Serves 6-8

4 large peaches
1 portion shortcrust pastry (see page 182)
1 oz (30 g) walnuts
1 oz (30 g) blanched almonds
1 oz (30 g) ground almonds
2 tbsp dark muscovado sugar
½ small orange
1 tbsp peach brandy or Marsala wine (optional)
½ oz (15 g) butter

Make the pastry in the usual way and line a 9 inch (23 cm) flan tin. Bake blind for 10-15 minutes in an oven preheated to Gas 5/375°F/190°, remove the beans and bake for a further 5 minutes, then allow to cool. Scald the peaches in boiling water, peel and halve them and remove the stones. Finely chop the nuts and mix with the ground almonds and sugar. Grate the rind from the orange and stir that in too.

Slice the peaches and arrange the slices in the pastry case. Sprinkle with the brandy or Marsala (alternatively use the juice from the orange). Sprinkle the nut topping all over the flan and dot with the butter. Preheat the grill and when really hot pop the flan under it for 5 minutes, until the topping is crisp and bubbling hot.

Poached Peaches with Blackberry Sauce

Here is a lovely dessert to serve at the end of summer, when the last peaches are still available cheaply and blackberries are also being harvested. It would make a good dessert for a dinner party, and can be prepared in advance. The sauce, incidentally, goes well with all sorts of fruits and desserts, and is a good way of using blackberries that are going a bit mushy. If you like you can thicken it slightly – return to the heat after sieving, add a teaspoon of cornflour dissolved in a tablespoon of water and stir till thickened.

Serves 4

5 large peaches
4 tsp fromage frais or Greek cow's yoghurt
½ pint (300 ml) clear apple juice
8 oz (225 g) blackberries
1 tbsp honey
2 tbsp brandy
1 tbsp finely chopped nuts

Scald the peaches in boiling water, dip into cold and peel them, before halving them and removing the stone. Chop one peach into small chunks and mix with the fromage frais or yoghurt. Bring the apple juice to the boil in a large saucepan, add the peach halves, cut side down, and poach for 3-5 minutes until just tender. Remove with a slotted spoon and arrange cut side up in a shallow glass dish.

Add the washed blackberries, honey and brandy to the apple juice and simmer for 5 minutes until the honey has dissolved and the blackberries are beginning to disintegrate. Taste and add extra honey if desired. Sieve the blackberries with the juices, throwing out any pulp left at the end.

Pile the yoghurt and peach mixture on to each half peach. Sprinkle with the nuts. Flood the dish with the sauce and spoon a little over the peaches. Chill before serving.

Spiced Bottled Peaches with Brandy

This is an excellent way of preserving peaches when they are at the height of their season, to be eaten later in the year, as part of your Christmas meal or just as a treat for dinner. You should use wide-necked Kilner jars with proper seals to store them in.

I always used to get excited as a child when I saw my mother's bottled peaches come down from the top shelf of the icy larder, for then I knew Christmas was just around the corner.

Makes 2

12 medium to large peaches
12-24 cloves
squeeze of lemon juice
1½ lb (670 g) unrefined
   granulated sugar

1½ pints (850 ml) water
2 inch (5 cm) stick cinnamon
few blades mace
½ pint (300 ml) brandy

Choose peaches that are not overripe. Dip into boiling water to loosen their skins, then peel. If they are too large to fit into the jars, halve and remove the stones. Prick them all over with a darning needle or similar implement and stick a clove into the stalk end (if they are halved stick the clove in near that end). To prevent the peach flesh discolouring while you peel the others, drop them into a bowl of cold water to which you have added a good squeeze of lemon juice.

Add the sugar to the water with the cinnamon and mace blades and stir over a gentle heat until the sugar has completely dissolved. Bring to the boil and boil rapidly for 2-3 minutes. Add the peaches, return to a simmer and cook for 5-10 minutes until the peaches are tender. Lift them out and pack into the clean jars. Pour over the brandy.

Cool the syrup and pour it over the peaches. Seal and store in a cool dry place out of the light.

Redcurrants

See Blackcurrants and Redcurrants, page 57.

Boned Chicken Stuffed with Redcurrants

Boned stuffed chicken not only looks impressive, but stretches to feed
more people, too, as the stuffing pads it out considerably. Here is a novel
redcurrant stuffing which looks particularly attractive when you slice the
chicken. You can either serve it cold for a summer dinner with salad, or
hot with roast potatoes.

Serves 6

4 lb (1.8 kg) chicken
10 oz (280 g) redcurrants
½ medium onion
1 oz (30 g) butter
2 tbsp clear honey
large pinch cinnamon

4 cloves
seasoning
1 heaped tbsp dry wholemeal
 breadcrumbs
2 tbsp dry vermouth
1 egg

First bone the chicken. This is not as hard as it sounds if you have a small
sharp knife. Cut off the wings at the first joint out from the body. Turn
the bird so the back (flat side) is facing you and cut with the knife
through the skin to the bone in a long line down the centre. Using short,
sharp strokes, work the flesh away from the bone on one side until you
reach the wing. Cut through the sinews at the wing joint and scrape the
flesh along the wing bone until you can pull it free.

   Continue working the flesh away from the body until you reach the
ball and socket joint where the leg meets the body. Cut through it and
sever the sinews attaching it, then scrape the flesh off until you arrive at
the joint with the drumstick. Cut the sinews again and scrape on down
the bone. Turn the leg inside out so it can lie inside the rolled up bird.
Repeat on the other side until your work is joined over the breast. It does
not really matter if it's a bit raggedy, but be careful not to pierce the skin
or the stuffing will ooze out.

   Wash the redcurrants and strip them off the stalks, then drain them
on kitchen paper. Chop the onion finely and sauté it in the butter for a
few minutes, add the redcurrants, honey, cinnamon, cloves and
seasoning and cook until the juice just begins to run. Soak the
breadcrumbs in the vermouth and stir into the mixture. Cool slightly and
add the beaten egg.

   Set the oven to Gas 4/350°F/180°C. Spread the stuffing over the inner
side of the boned chicken, leaving a clear border of about 1½ inches
(4 cm) round the edge. Fold one long side over the other to form a long,

plump sausage. Sew up the join with large stitches, using button thread and a big needle. Sew up the join where the large opening on the whole chicken was, as well.

Turn the chicken on to a sheet of greased silver foil, so the join is hidden. Bring the sides half-way up the chicken and lay another piece of silver foil on top, crimping the two edges together. Place in a roasting tin and cook in the oven for 1¾ hours. Thirty minutes before the end, remove the top piece of silver foil to allow the chicken to brown.

The meat will slice more easily when cold, but is equally good hot.

Redcurrants with Melon

This is a lovely summer fruit salad, which is very quick and easy to make. Remember to leave enough time for the sweet Sauternes wine to flavour the dish properly (about 1-2 hours). A melon baller is needed ideally, but if you don't have one just cut the melon into small chunks.

Serves 6
1 lb (450 g) redcurrants
2 Ogen or Charentais melons

¼-½ bottle Sauternes

Halve the melons and scoop out the seeds. Cut the flesh out with a melon baller, laying its flat edge against the melon flesh and then twisting it as if you were turning a key. Put all the melon balls into a glass dish and add the redcurrants, stripped off the stalks and lightly washed. Pour over the Sauternes, stir slightly and chill until ready to serve.

Layered Red Fruit Pudding

Anyone who is watching their weight will enjoy this, since it has all the delights of a fruit sundae with not nearly as many calories. You will find that the addition of the other ingredients means the redcurrants shouldn't need any sweetening, but put a small bowl of clear honey on the table for those who have a sweet tooth. The liqueur is optional but quite delicious !

Serves 4
1¼ lb (500 g) redcurrants
1 lb (450 g) strawberries or
  raspberries

1 lb (450 g) fromage frais
4 tsp crème de frais or crème de
  framboise liqueur

Wash and strip the redcurrants from their stalks, hull the strawberries or pick over the raspberries. Weigh out 4 oz (110 g) of redcurrants and mix them with the fromage frais in a liquidizer or food processor, or mash well with a fork or balloon whisk.

Take four individual small glass bowls. Divide the remaining redcurrants between them (saving just a few for final decoration), sprinkling them with the liqueur in the bottom of the dishes. Cover with half the fromage frais. For the next layer use all the raspberries or halved strawberries, and then cover with the rest of the fromage frais. Finish off with a few redcurrants and chill until ready to eat.

Redcurrant Cheesecake

This is an easy dessert to make, so long as you leave sufficient time for it to set. Do not put on the final redcurrants for decoration until shortly before serving, in order to make the finished appearance as neat as possible.

Serves 6-8

1¼ lb (550 g) redcurrants
8 oz (225 g) wholemeal digestive biscuits
3-4 oz (55-85 g) butter

7 oz (195 g) low-fat cream cheese
1 small tub (150 g) natural yoghurt
1 tbsp clear honey
0.4 oz (11g) sachet gelatine

Crush the digestive biscuits with a rolling pin. Melt the butter in a saucepan and stir in the biscuit crumbs until well coated, then transfer to an 8 inch (20 cm) cake tin with a removable bottom and press down well with your hand. Put into the freezer briefly to chill.

Strip the stalks from the redcurrants. Beat the cream cheese and yoghurt together until smooth then stir in 1 lb (450 g) of the redcurrants. Add the honey to a few tablespoons of water in a small saucepan, sprinkle the gelatine over, and leave to sponge. When it has absorbed some of the water, heat very gently until dissolved and then stir into the cream cheese and redcurrant mixture.

Turn on to the biscuit base and leave in the fridge to set. To decorate arrange the reserved redcurrants at regular intervals round the top edge of the cheesecake, and pile a few in the centre.

Redcurrant Sauce

A homemade fruit sauce such as this goes very well with halved peaches, ice-creams, and other summery desserts. If you have sufficient redcurrants to freeze, this works equally well made with frozen ones.

1 lb (450 g) redcurrants, weighed after stripping
4 cloves
pinch cinnamon

1-2 tbsp clear honey
1 tsp cornflour
2 tbsp water

Put the redcurrants in a saucepan with the spices and a spoonful or two of water and cook gently until the juices begin to run (about 5-10 minutes). Push through a sieve (pick out the cloves) into another small pan, add the honey and cook gently, stirring, until the honey has dissolved. Taste for sweetness then mix the cornflour with the water, pour into the sauce and return to the boil. As soon as the sauce is thick remove it from the heat.

Redcurrant and Raspberry Jam

These two fruits go well together in jam, which is a godsend if you have a fruit cage overflowing with the two crops, since they ripen at the same time. Raspberries do not have a very high pectin content, which means it is more difficult to obtain a good 'set' when using them in jam, but the addition of redcurrants solves the problem.

Makes about 6 lb (2.7 kg)
1 lb (450 g) redcurrants
2 lb (900 g) raspberries
½ pint (300 ml) water

3 lb (1.35 kg) unrefined granulated
    sugar

Strip the redcurrants from their stalks and simmer them in the water for 10 minutes or so until soft. Push through a sieve back into the pan and add the raspberries. Cook for about 5 minutes, then add the sugar and stir until dissolved. Increase the heat and boil rapidly until setting point is reached (see Jams and Jellies). Pour into clean pots and seal and store in the usual way.

   If you don't like the small pips found in raspberries, you can add the raspberries before sieving the redcurrants, simmer a few minutes and then push the whole lot through a sieve. Stir in the sugar and proceed as above.

Redcurrant Jelly

Redcurrants make a particularly good jelly, traditionally served as an accompaniment to lamb, but also excellent with venison and other game. The fruit is high in pectin, so setting point is reached quite quickly and you can use the double extract method. It is not necessary to strip the berries from the stalks before making the jelly, which saves a considerable amount of time.

3 lb (1.35 kg) redcurrants
2¼ pints (1.3 litres) water

unrefined granulated sugar

Wash the fruit and put it in a large pan with 1½ pints (850 ml) of the water. Simmer for about 45 minutes or until the currants are really soft and pulpy. Strain through a jelly bag for an hour, then return the fruit to the pan with the remaining ¾ pint (425 ml) water. Simmer a further 30 minutes then strain through the bag overnight.

Measure the juice and mix it with 1 lb (450 g) sugar to each pint (550 ml) liquid. Heat gently, stirring, until the sugar is completely dissolved, then boil rapidly until setting point is reached, about 10 minutes.

Remove from the heat, skim off any scum and pot into small warm jars. Cover, leave to grow cold in the usual way (see Jams and Jellies), then label and store in a cool, dry place.

Salmon

Scotch salmon is one of Britain's best raw ingredients, served with varying degrees of skill and attention in many restaurants and homes. At the start of the season (February) it is ruinously expensive. Even if you catch your own, the cost of the fishing rights pound for pound put it in the caviar class. In summer, when netting is allowed, the price falls to within range of more pockets and affords the opportunity to enjoy it to the full. However, even salmon can pall if you have too much, particularly if you buy or are given a whole fish, which can be very large. This is the time to vary the menu from simple poached salmon and to try some more inventive ways of serving it.

Many people are confused about the different types of salmon. The true wild variety has a more pointed nose from annually battling upriver to spawn, a wider tail and a large fin in the middle of the back. Farmed salmon, reared in sea corrals, possesses a blunter snout and often has black spots on the skin.

All salmon should be gutted and scaled before using – the weights given here are for ready-to-cook, rather than ungutted, fish. Choose ones that are stiff and have a bright sheen to the eye and skin, and eat them as quickly as possible. Most households buy steaks (allow one each) or a piece, which you can ask the fishmonger to fillet.

Gravad Lax with Dill Sauce

This is a superb Scandinavian dish which I almost prefer to smoked salmon. The fish is marinated for several days (anything between two and five) and then sliced slightly more thickly than smoked salmon. It is refreshing and wonderfully moist. Use fresh not frozen salmon.

Serves 6-8 as a starter, 4 as a main course.

2½ lb (1.1 kg) piece fresh salmon	**Sauce**
1 tbsp brandy	2 tbsp mild German mustard
1 tbsp sunflower oil	1 egg yolk
1½ tbsp unrefined granulated	seasoning
sugar	6 tbsp olive oil
2 tbsp sea salt	3 tbsp fresh chopped dill
2 tbsp black peppercorns	3 tbsp white wine vinegar
1 large bunch fresh dill	

Fillet the fish by cutting it in half lengthways and removing the central bone with a sharp flexible filleting knife. Sprinkle the oil and brandy over the two fillets and rub in well. Mix the sugar, salt and crushed black pepper together and sprinkle over the salmon.

Divide the dill, unchopped, into three and lay one-third at the bottom of a gratin dish. Lay one of the salmon pieces, skin side down, on top, cover with more dill and sandwich with the other salmon fillet skin side up. Strew the rest of the dill over the top, cover with a double piece of silver foil, then put a plate on top and weigh down with full tins or other heavy objects. Put the dish in the fridge and leave for 2 days, basting the salmon every 12 hours or so with the marinade.

To make the dill sauce, beat the mustard, egg yolk and seasoning together and then beat in the oil gradually as you would for mayonnaise. When thick and well emulsified, whisk in the dill and vinegar. Slice the salmon in long horizontal strips and serve with lemon wedges and thin slices of wholemeal bread. Hand the sauce separately.

Hot Poached Salmon with Watercress Sauce

Classic poached salmon is justly one of Britain's most famous dishes. Few people these days have a fish kettle, which was the traditional way of cooking a salmon, but the method used below solves this problem while still keeping the fish moist. Ask your fishmonger for some bones to make the fish stock with, or use salmon bones from the rest of the fish, if you are dealing with one you have caught.

Serves 6-8

3 lb (1.35 kg) piece salmon	2 oz (55 g) soft butter
2 tbsp sunflower oil	3 inch (8 cm) piece cucumber
2-3 bayleaves	½ oz (15 g) unbleached plain
few black peppercorns	flour
½ lemon	½ pint (300 ml) fish stock
1 large glass dry white wine	1 tsp anchovy essence
	black pepper
Sauce	squeeze lemon juice
2 bunches watercress	

The salmon will have been cleaned when it was divided into pieces. Oil a large piece of silver foil and lay the fish on top. Insert the bayleaves, black peppercorns and sliced half lemon into the belly of the fish, raise the sides of the foil and pour in the wine. Seal the envelope by crimping the edges of the foil together and lay it on a baking sheet. Cook in an oven preheated to Gas 4/350°F/180°C for 45-50 minutes.

To make the sauce, wash the watercress well under cold running water and cut off the stalks. Drop it into a pan of boiling water and simmer for a few minutes until tender. Drain well and purée in a food processor or liquidizer with 1½ oz (45 g) of the butter, then scrape out and set aside. Chop the cucumber very finely by hand or machine and simmer it a few minutes in its own juices in a saucepan. Set aside.

Make a roux by melting the rest of the butter and adding the flour. Gradually blend in the fish stock until you have a smooth sauce. Add the anchovy essence, season with black pepper and simmer for 5-10 minutes, then leave until just before serving.

Open up the silver foil containing the salmon and gently scrape a piece of skin away up near the back bone – if the flesh is pale pink the fish is ready. While it is being dished up, reheat the sauce and drop the watercress butter in, piece by piece, beating well. Don't let the sauce boil. Then reheat the cucumber, stir it into the sauce, add a squeeze of lemon juice and serve in a warmed sauceboat with the fish.

Salmon Steaks Florentine

Salmon is at its cheapest while summer spinach is still plentiful. This is a simple dish but it needs a little planning in order to have everything ready at the same time – I would advise against preceding it with a first course for that reason.

Serves 4

4 salmon steaks
3 lb (1.35 kg) spinach
2½ fl.oz (75 ml) double cream

seasoning
1-2 oz (30-55 g) butter
hollandaise sauce (see page 179)

Wash the spinach really well and put it into a large pan with no added water, to cook for about 5-10 minutes until tender. Stir it occasionally to ensure it does not stick to the bottom of the pan. Drain it and press well between two plates to squeeze out all excess moisture, then chop it roughly and mix with the cream and seasoning in a saucepan, not over the heat. Set aside. Reduce the vinegar for the hollandaise sauce and cut the butter for it into small pieces. All this can be done in advance.

Melt the butter in a small saucepan while you line the grill pan with a piece of aluminium foil. Arrange the salmon steaks on top and brush them with a little of the melted butter. Preheat the grill until you have a steady, moderate heat and cook the steaks under it for about 4 minutes each side, brushing with more butter to prevent them from drying out. While the steaks are cooking make the hollandaise sauce, and gently heat the creamed spinach in a saucepan.

Cover the bottom of a warmed serving dish with the spinach, arrange the grilled salmon on top and pour the sauce over. Serve immediately.

Koulibiac

This splendid Russian dish creates the centrepiece for a hot buffet or dinner party. All the preparation can be done ahead and the dish kept in the fridge until the final baking, but remember in that case to leave it at room temperature for half-an-hour or more beforehand or the chilled centre will not get really hot.

Serves 6-8

1½ lb (670 g) filleted salmon
1 lb (450 g) packet puff pastry
8 oz (225 g) button mushrooms
2 medium onions
2-3 oz (55-85 g) unsalted butter
6 oz (170 g) brown rice

2 tbsp fresh chopped dill or
   2 tsp dried
3 tbsp fresh chopped parsley
seasoning
2 eggs
½ pint (300 ml) dry white wine
beaten egg

Slice the mushrooms finely, chop the onions. Heat the butter in a saucepan and sweat the onions until soft, then add the mushrooms and cook until the juices run. Season well and set aside.

Cook the rice in water or stock until tender, drain and mix with the dill, parsley and seasoning. Hardboil the eggs, then shell and slice them. Slice the salmon thickly and simmer it in a pan with the white wine for about 5-8 minutes, it should still be quite rosy. Strain.

Roll out just less than half the pastry into an oblong shape. Put half the rice on it leaving a border of about 1½ inches (3.5 cm) round the edges. Arrange the fish on top, then the sliced egg and the mushroom and onion mixture. Cover with the remaining rice. Roll out the rest of the pastry into a slightly larger oblong, brush round the rim of the pastry containing the salmon with water or milk and drape the second piece over the top. Press down well to seal, then tuck underneath. Brush the entire surface with beaten egg, including any leaves or decoration you may care to make out of the leftover pastry, and bake in an oven preheated to Gas 6/400°F/200°C for 45 minutes, covering the pastry with silverfoil if it starts to over-brown. Serve sliced.

Salmon Kedgeree

Kedgeree was originally an Indian dish, brought back from India in the days of the Raj. It was first known as khichiri, used mainly smoked fish and was fairly spicy. This is a more subtle version, which is an excellent way of using up a little cooked salmon, either as a supper or brunch dish. Be careful how you cook the rice or the dish will end up stodgy – I find the easiest kind to use is the easy cook brown rice, which is lighter.

Serves 6

12 oz (335 g) cooked salmon	3 oz (85 g) butter
1 lb (450 g) brown rice	pinch cayenne
2 hardboiled eggs	seasoning
1 medium onion	1 tbsp fresh chopped parsley

Put the rice on to cook. Shell and chop the eggs. Chop the onion and soften it in the butter. Flake the salmon carefully and add it with the egg, cayenne and seasoning, and heat together gently. Drain the rice and add it to the salmon, heat through and transfer to a warmed serving dish. It should be quite buttery. Sprinkle with the parsley and serve.

Tomatoes

If a single vegetable could epitomize the philosophy behind this book, it would surely be the tomato. Expensive and rather tasteless out of season, tomatoes suddenly overflow the market stalls in late summer, while home-grown ones ripen by the dozen in the greenhouse and overwhelm you with their abundance. Even with the help of your fridge, you can't store tomatoes for long without their going squishy. Slightly damaged ones are often to be picked up for a song at the greengrocer, and again the problem is how to serve them before they deteriorate too far. I have included here my favourite and much-used recipes to solve this seasonal dilemma.

Despite their current profusion, tomatoes have had only a short association with this country. Although I knew that the conquistadors originally brought them over from Latin America, where they had been domesticated in Mexico by the Aztecs (who called them *tomatl*), I was amazed when I learnt that they only appeared on British tables in any serious way early this century. The Americans started growing them around 1835, while they had been popular in Spain and Italy since the eighteenth century. The early ones brought back were golden, which is perhaps why they were first called love apples and used more as a decoration than in the kitchen, but when the red varieties were introduced they began to appear in recipe books.

Different varieties are more suited to different ways of eating them. Plum tomatoes, for example, which are the sort used for canning, are best for sauces and concentrated purées, while others are best for salads. Unfortunately in England, commercially grown ones offer little choice and have been standardized out of all recognition from the type you can grow in your own plot. However small your garden is, it really is worth giving over a sheltered sunny spot or a corner of your greenhouse to a few tomato plants. Alternatively make use of the increasing number of farms offering pick-your-own crops, which in the case of tomatoes is a quick and easy way of obtaining them at a low price. Otherwise you must rely on the rather bland sort sold in shops, usually Moneymakers, which are high-cropping but lack flavour.

Many recipes make use of tomatoes among their main ingredients. See, for example, Broad Bean Stuffed Tomatoes, Lamb and Runner Bean Casserole, Curried Cauliflower and the sauce for Spinach and Cream Cheese Ramekins; Cauliflower Provençal, French Beans provençal and Jerusalem Artichokes Provençal; and aubergine dishes such as Veronese Aubergine Gratin, Ratatouille, Spicy Aubergines and Stuffed Aubergines.

Hummus-Stuffed Tomatoes

Filling hollowed-out tomatoes with this popular and delicious Middle Eastern pâté is a perfect way to use up the mass of small tomatoes left in the greenhouse at the end of summer, which ripen in clouds without ever growing to normal size. Those relying on shops can either hunt down the little cherry tomatoes, or halve normal-sized ones. A piping bag makes the stuffing process easier, but isn't essential, while a melon baller makes the task of scraping out the insides of the tomato much quicker. They make an excellent snack served with drinks.

Makes about 20-30

2 lb (900 g) small tomatoes	no more than 2½ fl.oz (75 ml)
5 oz (140 g) dried chickpeas	olive oil
2 lemons	little water or milk
2 cloves garlic	2 tbsp fresh chopped parsley
black pepper	

Soak the chickpeas overnight in cold water, or pour boiling water over and soak for an hour. Drain and put the peas into fresh water, with no salt, and boil for 1-1½ hours until tender.

Meanwhile cut the tops off the tomatoes, or halve them if they are the slightly bigger variety. Using a melon baller or sharp-edged teaspoon, scrape the pips and flesh out of the inside of each tomato, then leave it to drain, cut side down, on kitchen paper. This is to mop up the surplus juice which otherwise gets mixed in with the hummus and makes it rather watery.

Purée the drained chickpeas in a blender or food processor with the juice of 2 lemons, the crushed garlic cloves, lots of black pepper and the olive oil. You will probably need to add a little water or milk as well to achieve the right smooth consistency. Fill the tomato shells with the hummus, either with a teaspoon or using a piping bag. Scatter with chopped parsley.

Andalusian Gazpacho

When my sister lived in Andalusia she used to make this cold uncooked soup without the aid of machines, which meant lengthy chopping of everything and then passing it all through a hand-Mouli. With a liquidizer it can be made in seconds, but remember to leave plenty of time for it to chill – at least three hours. If you are using a food processor, which doesn't purée things so well, process the 'drier' ingredients first (onion, bread, green pepper), before adding the tomatoes and cucumber.

Serves 4-6

2½ lb (1.1 kg) ripe or over-ripe
   tomatoes
1 green pepper
1 small onion
3 slices bread
½ cucumber
seasoning

small clove garlic
1 tbsp wine vinegar
2 tbsp olive oil
up to 1 tbsp tomato purée
   (optional)
olive oil for frying

Deseed the green pepper and cut it into pieces. Add it to the liquidizer with the peeled quartered onion, the tomatoes (halved or quartered if large), one slice of bread, broken into pieces and the crust removed, two-thirds of the cucumber cut into chunks, the seasoning and peeled garlic clove. You will probably need to do all this in two batches to avoid over-filling the machine. Liquidize until really smooth and pour into a large bowl or soup tureen. Add the vinegar and oil and up to 2 wineglasses of water – the whole lot should equal about 2¾ pints (1.5 litres). Chill.

Dice the rest of the cucumber and the bread, frying the bread cubes in oil until golden brown to make croûtons. Hand these separately when you serve the soup, to be sprinkled on top.

If the tomatoes are rather bland, use tomato juice from a tin or carton in place of the water and add a little tomato purée for extra flavour.

Tomato and Orange Soup

The wonderful taste of ripe tomatoes is brought out beautifully in a soup. The tomatoes on sale most of the year in Britain – tasteless examples of the way market gardening has been geared towards appearance and standard sizes rather than flavour – are not much use for this recipe. Home-grown tomatoes are best, although you may alternatively find a good local outlet during the time when tomatoes are at their cheapest which sells what I call 'the real thing'.

Serves 4

2 lb (900 g) ripe tomatoes	seasoning
1 medium onion	1 tbsp fresh chopped basil or
1 small clove garlic	pinch dried
1 tbsp sunflower oil	bayleaf
1-2 tsp tomato purée (optional)	1 orange
1 pint (550 ml) chicken stock	

Skin the tomatoes and chop them roughly. Chop the onion and sauté it lightly with the garlic in the oil for 5 minutes. Add the tomatoes and stir for another couple of minutes, stirring in the tomato purée if you feel the tomatoes are not as flavoursome as they might be. Pour in the stock and season lightly, adding the basil and bayleaf. Bring to the boil and simmer, covered, for 20 minutes.

Liquidize and taste. If the soup has a really strong flavour, add the juice and grated rind of the whole orange. If you think this may overwhelm the tomato, add these gradually until the right balance is achieved.

Tomato Ice

For a change, serve tomatoes as a first course frozen into a kind of sorbet. It sounds strange, but is surprisingly popular. Choose tomatoes that are ripe and deep red, or the end-result will look a bit anaemic.

Serves 6

1 lb (450 g) ripe tomatoes	2 tsp tomato purée
1 stick celery	seasoning
2 spring onions	juice of ½ lemon
2-3 tbsp tomato ketchup	just over ¼ pint (75 ml)
few drops Tabasco sauce	whipping cream

Peel the tomatoes and scrape out the pips into a sieve with a little bowl underneath. Press the seeds against the mesh to extract the juice and then discard them. Finely chop the celery and the white part of the spring onions. Put the tomatoes, the juice, chopped vegetables and all the other ingredients except the cream into a liquidizer and process until smooth. Whip the cream and fold it into the tomato mixture. Pour into individual ramekins and freeze.

Transfer the dishes from the freezer to the fridge about 1 hour before serving. Leave at room temperature for the last 5 minutes and serve decorated with a twist of sliced lemon and a fresh basil leaf, or a little watercress.

Tomato and Mozzarella Salad

There is a world of difference between a really good tomato salad with herbs and lemony dressing, and the few quartered tomatoes with some raw onion seen all too often on buffet tables. Personally I don't like raw onion in many things, particularly not scattered over delicious garden-fresh tomatoes, but I concede that this may be a matter of taste. Far nicer is to include some slices of mild creamy Mozzarella cheese, some fresh herbs and a zip of lemon to make a really tasty first course.

Serves 4

6 medium tomatoes
8 oz (225 g) Mozzarella cheese
½ lemon
3 tbsp olive oil
seasoning
bunch fresh basil or chives

Skin the tomatoes – this in itself makes an ordinary salad special because of the immediate change in texture. Simply dip them in a pan of boiling water for the count of 10, plunge into cold and peel the skins off with a small knife. Slice the cheese across into thin rectangles and the tomatoes not too thinly. Arrange the different slices alternately in two or three rows down a shallow gratin dish. Grate the lemon rind and scatter over the top.

Squeeze the juice from the lemon and beat it into the oil with some seasoning. Pour this over the tomatoes and scatter the chopped basil or chives all over. Leave to stand at room temperature for half-an-hour or more to draw out the different flavours before serving. A good simple snack is to lay any leftovers from this salad, already dressed, between pieces of French bread, pressing down firmly so the tomato juice seeps into the bread.

Tomatoes Stuffed with Minty Peas

Bright red tomatoes filled with a purée of garden peas mixed with a little potato and freshly chopped mint makes an excellent accompaniment to roast lamb or lightly poached salmon. A perfect summer dish. The quantity below gives one filled tomato each, those with good appetites can easily put away two.

Serves 4

4 fairly large tomatoes (about
    12 oz/670 g total)
4 oz (110 g) shelled peas
½ medium potato

½ oz (15 g) butter
1 tbsp fresh chopped mint or
    pinch dried
black pepper

Cut off the tops of the tomatoes, reserving these for later, and scoop out the insides with a melon baller or sharp-edged teaspoon. If the base is very rounded and you find the tomato won't sit flat, shave a sliver off, without breaking through the tomato wall.

Simmer the peas for 3 minutes or so until tender. Peel and boil the potato until cooked. Drain the vegetables and while still hot purée them in a food processor, or mash together really well, with the butter and mint. Add a generous amount of black pepper and pile into the tomato shells. Replace with the little lids and bake at Gas 6/400°F/200°C for 10-15 minutes until the tomatoes are cooked, but not overdone or they will fall apart. If you want them to look really special, you can pipe the pea purée in with a piping bag, using a starred nozzle, in which case you will not need to replace the lids.

All-Purpose Tomato Sauce

This is my basic tomato sauce which I use for everything. It takes no time to prepare and although at some times of the year I use tinned tomatoes, instead of the expensive and rather tasteless imported ones which are all that are available, in season it tastes infinitely better made with fresh ripe ones.

You can use it as a basis for casseroles or as a pasta sauce, to pour over vegetables like cauliflower or for cooking fish like red mullet or cod.

1 lb (450 g) ripe tomatoes
½ medium onion
1 large clove garlic
1 tbsp olive oil
1 level tbsp wholemeal flour
1 tsp tomato purée

pinch thyme
pinch basil
2 tbsp red wine
bayleaf
seasoning

Chop the onion and skin the tomatoes in the usual way, before chopping them roughly as well. Heat the oil in a saucepan (a non-stick one is a good idea) and sauté the onion with the crushed garlic until soft but not brown. Stir in the flour and tomato purée and cook for half a minute. (If you are using tomatoes that taste rather bland, add extra purée.) Add the tomatoes, crushing them with a potato masher as they begin to soften. Add the herbs, wine and bayleaf and season well, then cover and simmer over a gentle heat for 20 minutes at least, stirring just once or twice. Remove the bayleaf and use or freeze.

Tomato Chutney

If you grow your own tomatoes, there is always a moment near the end of the season when you have so many you don't know what to do with them. This is the moment to make large quantities of chutney. Since the glut often coincides with the time when courgettes are also very plentiful and tend to grow unnoticed to almost marrow-like proportions, you can use them in the chutney too.

Makes 5 Kilner jars

5 lb (2.25 kg) ripe tomatoes
2 lb (900 g) overgrown courgettes
1 lb (450 g) onions
2 tsp ground allspice (or ½ tsp
   each cinnamon, cayenne,
   paprika, ginger

1 tbsp salt
¾ pint (425 ml) malt vinegar
4 tbsp clear honey

Skin the tomatoes in the normal way. Quarter them and put into a large preserving pan with the chopped onion. Top and tail the courgettes and if the seeds are very large, scoop them out before dicing and adding to the tomatoes with the spices, salt and a little of the vinegar. Cook for 30-60 minutes until all the ingredients are soft and pulpy.

At this stage add the rest of the vinegar and the honey, stir until all the honey has dissolved, then boil until the chutney is thick and jam-like. Pour into sterilized jars and seal in the normal way. This chutney should be cooked long and slowly over a low heat to obtain the right smooth texture, and is better eaten after it has been stored for a month or so.

Green Tomato Chutney

At the end of the tomato-growing season there are always quite a few tomatoes that have failed to ripen before the early autumn weather puts an end to the summer. This is an ideal way to make use of all those that would otherwise be wasted.

Makes 2-3 Kilner jars

2 lb (900 g) green tomatoes
8 oz (225 g) onions
1 cooking apple
2 tsp ground allspice (or ½ tsp
   each cinnamon, cayenne,
   paprika, ginger

1 tsp salt
1 tsp mustard powder
8 oz (225 g) sultanas
½ pint (300 ml) malt vinegar

Soften the onions in a large pan in a tablespoon or so of the vinegar while you slice the tomatoes and peel, core and chop the apple. When the onions are nearly soft add all the other ingredients except the remaining vinegar. Simmer until the whole lot is quite soft, stirring occasionally.

Add the rest of the vinegar and boil until the chutney reaches a jam-like consistency. Pour into jars and seal in the usual way before storing in a cool, dry place.

AUTUMN

Apples

As October approaches, the new crop of British apples appears in the shops by the barrowload. Those who have an apple tree in the garden, whether one giving cooking or eating apples, will be inundated by the crop. There are a dozen delicious ways to use cooking apples other than simply baking them stuffed, and eaters too can be used in recipes as well as being enjoyed by themselves after a meal or as a snack. Eating apples can also be used to help sweeten dishes instead of sugar. Cook them down to a purée first, and add to taste. The purée can be frozen in small amounts to be taken out and used for this purpose as and when needed.

Until the importing of fruit from the Southern hemisphere began in a serious way, apples were the only fresh fruit available through the winter and it was common for most households to lay down a stock in an outside shed. If you have an apple tree in your garden, it is still worth doing this with the early autumn crop. Choose blemish-free fruit (not windfalls), wrap each one loosely in newspaper and lay on slatted wooden trays in a frost-free shed or garage. Lofts or cellars are not always suitable as they can be rather warm.

Apples are one of the oldest and most popular fruits outside the tropics. There were around twenty varieties recorded in Roman times, and thousands of different ones known today. However, the most common kinds available in our shops are Bramley cooking apples, most of which are native-grown, and eating apples like Cox's Orange Pippin or Russet, which are two excellent English varieties. The infamous Golden Delicious is a rather bland, watery but consistently reliable apple, originally from France, which has flooded the British market, much to the fury of the Kent apple farmers. Other varieties are Worcester Pearmain with a shiny red skin, which can be quite good but often has a rather woolly flesh, and Granny Smith, which is very crisp but sometimes a bit underripe and sour.

Although cooking apples cannot be eaten raw, being very sour, eaters can quite happily be cooked. Cookers tend to break down easily to a purée, which makes them especially good for chutneys, sauces, and fillings.

For other recipes using apples, see Blackberry and Apple Jam and Blackberry and Apple Pasty, and Rhubarb, Apple and Almond Soup.

Curried Apple Soup

This is a delicious and unusual soup that is excellent served cold as a prelude to a curry meal, or hot as part of a lunch of cold meats and pickles. It is a clever way of using cooking apples other than as a dessert. I make it using mild curry powder, but if you happen to have only medium or hot in your storecupboard, adjust the quantity to a dessertspoon or teaspoon accordingly.

Serves 6
2 lb (900 g) cooking apples
1 medium onion
½ oz (15 g) butter
1 level tbsp mild curry powder
1¾ pints (1 litre) chicken stock

bayleaf
1 tbsp clear honey
black pepper
2½ fl. oz (75 ml) single cream

Peel, quarter, core and slice the apples. Slice the onion and cook it in the butter for about 5 minutes. Stir in the curry powder and cook a further minute or two, then add the sliced apples, stock, bayleaf and honey. Bring to the boil and simmer, covered, for 10 minutes until the apples are really soft.

Remove the bayleaf and liquidize the soup. Taste and add a little more curry powder if you feel it needs it. Remember that freshly stirred in curry powder takes about 10 minutes to develop its full flavour, so don't overdo it. Season with black pepper and stir in the cream.

Either reheat or chill well before serving.

Cornish Apple and Lamb Pie

If it's the end of the week and you want a cheap, filling meal that is still a bit out of the ordinary, try this old Cornish recipe. Served with potatoes and a good green vegetable like broccoli, it will stretch to feed six.

Serves 4

1¼ lb (550 g) lamb shoulder fillet
1 lb (450 g) cooking apples
1 medium onion
1 tbsp clear honey
3 tbsp freshly chopped parsley
pinch thyme
black pepper

½ pint (300 ml) lamb or chicken
  stock

Shortcrust pastry
4 oz (110 g) wholemeal flour
2 oz (55 g) unbleached plain flour
3 oz (85 g) butter
2 tbsp cold water

Make the pastry in the usual way, in a food processor or by hand, and leave it to chill in the fridge.

Trim any large pieces of fat from the lamb, but leave the little ones, and cube the meat. Peel, quarter, core and slice the apples. Slice the onion. Arrange a layer of apple over the base of an oval pie dish about 8-10 inches (20-25 cm) long, dribble over a little honey, then put in half the meat and sliced onion. Sprinkle with the herbs, season well with black pepper and repeat.

Pour in the stock, which shouldn't be steaming hot or it will soften the butter in the pastry before it gets into the oven. Roll out the pastry, brush some water round the rim of the pie dish and cover with the pastry, pressing down well. Knead the offcuts together, roll out and cut strips just wide enough to go all round the pastry rim. Moisten the rim with water and press the pastry strips down on top. This will prevent it shrinking away from the sides of the dish while cooking.

Brush the pie with beaten egg and bake in an oven preheated to Gas 7/425°F/220°C for 10 minutes, then lower the heat to Gas 5/375°F/170°C and leave for a further 30-40 minutes. Once the pastry is browned, cover it with a piece of aluminium foil.

Pork Fillet with Apple and Mushrooms

Although most of the cooking for this dish must be done at the last minute, it is very quick to prepare. Pork fillet is expensive, but once beaten out as shown below, it goes a long way, so you don't need very much per head.

Serves 4

3 Cox or Russet apples
1 lb (450 g) pork fillet in one
  piece (pork tenderloin)
3 tbsp olive oil
juice of 1 lemon
black pepper
1 medium onion

4 oz (110 g) mushrooms
squeeze lemon juice
1 large clove garlic
2 tbsp sunflower oil
1 oz (30 g) butter
small carton (150 g)
  natural yoghurt
1 tbsp fresh chopped parsley

Slice the pork fillet thinly across its width, then group 2-3 pieces together under a piece of wet greaseproof paper and flatten by gently beating with a rolling pin. Repeat until all the pieces are beaten out (they will increase considerably in size) and then transfer them to a shallow dish. Pour over the olive oil and lemon juice, sprinkle with freshly ground black pepper and leave to marinade for 1-3 hours.

Slice the onion and the mushrooms. Peel, quarter, core and thickly slice the apples and drop them in a bowl of water with a good squeeze of lemon juice to prevent them from discolouring. Sauté the onion in the oil with the crushed garlic in a large frying pan for a minute or two, add the mushroom, lower the heat and cover with a lid. Drain the marinade liquid off the pork.

Remove the cooked mushroom and onion to an oval serving plate, arranging it down one side, and keep warm in the oven. Turn up the heat, add the pork pieces and sauté until cooked (this will take virtually no time, they are so thin). You may have to do this in two batches. Arrange the pork in overlapping slices down the centre of the serving plate and return to the oven. Drain the apple slices and fry them in the butter over a high heat until golden brown on both sides. Arrange them down the opposite side of the plate from the mushrooms and keep warm.

Quickly pour the yoghurt into the pan, scrape up any meaty juices and pour over the pork when it is hot. Do not allow to boil or it will curdle, which does not affect the taste but spoils the appearance somewhat. Sprinkle with chopped parsley and serve.

Apple and Stilton Strudel

You can be guaranteed this dish will be a real winner. It is easy to make, easy to cook, and yet looks and tastes wonderful. I am not one of those cooks who is prepared to spend the time required to make my own strudel pastry. It is a highly skilled technique and not always successful for those new to it. Commercially bought filo pastry is a very acceptable substitute. This is available frozen from Greek grocers and Middle Eastern stores, and from some major supermarkets. Buy it when you see it and keep in the freezer.

Serves 6

12 oz (335 g) cooking apples
6 oz (170 g) filo pastry
3 oz (85 g) fresh wholemeal
  breadcrumbs
2 oz (55 g) unsalted butter
4 oz (110 g) Stilton cheese

2 oz (55 g) shelled hazlenuts
½ lemon
unsalted butter for oiling pastry
  layers
2 tbsp clear honey

Fry the breadcrumbs in the unsalted butter (they serve to soak up the apple juices while cooking and thereby prevent the dish from becoming watery). Chop the Stilton and the nuts, grate the lemon rind.

Weigh out the pastry, roll up the unwanted sheets and return them in their plastic bag and carton to the freezer. Take one of the weighed sheets and lay it on the work surface. Brush with melted unsalted butter and lay another piece on top. Repeat until all the layers are used up. Then sprinkle half the breadcrumbs all over the pastry, leaving a 1½ inch (4 cm) border round the edges. Peel, quarer, core and roughly chop the apples and lay them down the middle. Dribble the honey over the apples and scatter the remaining breadcrumbs on top with the Stilton, nuts and lemon rind.

Roll up the strudel from one short end to the other, and tuck in the edges. Place on a greased baking tray with the join underneath, then brush with melted butter. The dish can be prepared in advance up to this stage, but cover it with a damp cloth to prevent the pastry from drying out, and remoisten the cloth when necessary.

Bake in an oven preheated to Gas 7/425°F/220°C for 10 minutes, then lower to Gas 6/400°F/200°C and leave a further 30 minutes or until the pastry is golden brown. Serve hot or cold, with or without cream.

French Apple Flan

I have lost count of the number of times I have eaten this on the Continent – and of the number of times I tried to reproduce it in my own kitchen. Somehow it never quite worked, but after numerous experiments and variations I finally got it right. The secret, I found, is in which way you slice the apple – it should be round through its 'equator' rather than from top to bottom. This gives better bulk and an attractive, ordered appearance to the finished dish.

I have used three parts wholemeal flour to one part white here, which gives a healthy crust without being too heavyweight.

Serves 6-8

2½ lb (1.1 kg) Cox's apples
squeeze lemon juice
1-2 tbsp light muscovado or
    unrefined granulated sugar
3 tbsp apricot jam
1-2 tbsp lemon juice

Pastry
6 oz (170 g) wholemeal flour
2 oz (55 g) unbleached plain flour
2 oz (55 g) unrefined granulated
    sugar
4 oz (110 g) butter
2-3 tbsp cold water

First make the pastry in the usual way, either by hand or in a food processor, adding the sugar to the flour with the butter. Roll out and cut to line a 9 inch (23 cm) fluted flan dish, with a removable base. Chill for 30 minutes, then bake blind in an oven preheated to Gas 7/425°F/220°C for 10 minutes. Remove the paper and beans after this time and bake a further 5 minutes

Peel the apples and drop them whole into a bowl of water to which you have added a good squeeze of lemon juice. This prevents them from discolouring. When the flan case has been partly baked, take out each apple one by one, core it and then halve it from top to bottom. Place the flat side on the chopping board and slice across each half thinly so you end up with lots of C-shaped pieces.

Arrange these closely overlapping in the dish – there should be sufficient apples to make two layers. Do not space them too far apart or they will collapse during cooking. Sprinkle the surface with a spoonful or two of sugar and bake in a preheated oven at Gas 5-6/375-400°F/190-200°C for 20-30 minutes until the edges of the apples are just browning. If you think the apples are cooked enough before their edges have browned, finish off briefly under a hot grill, taking care not to burn the pastry.

Heat the jam and lemon juice gently in a saucepan and brush liberally over the flan, including the top edge of the pastry. Leave to grow cold, then remove the outer metal rim and slice the flan.

Apple Chutney

However much your household may like piccalilli and other fiery chutneys, it is always a good idea to have a store of something like this apple one – fairly mild and universally popular.

Makes about 5 lb (2.25 kg)
3½ (1.55 kg) cooking apples
8 oz (225 g) carrots
1 lb (450 g) onions
1 pint (550 ml) malt vinegar
4 oz (110 g) raisins

1 dsp dry mustard
1 tsp cayenne pepper
1 tsp ground ginger
4 tbsp clear honey

Peel, quarter, core and chop the apples. Trim and grate the carrots and chop the onions. Simmer for an hour in a large preserving pan, uncovered, with the vinegar, raisins, mustard and spices till thick and soft, stirring occasionally. Add the honey, stir till it has dissolved and simmer a further 30 minutes.

Spoon into warm, clean jars and seal while still hot. Store in a cool dry place for several months to allow the full flavour to develop before eating. If properly sealed this chutney will keep for a year or more.

Apple and Basil Jelly

Autumn heralds the end of the fresh herbs season for most people, unless you are successful at growing them indoors (something which is rarely possible unless you have a very sunny window ledge). Fresh basil is a delicious and useful herb to have throughout the summer, especially good in salads. Here is a way of enjoying it in the winter, by gathering the last of its leaves and combining them with a windfall of cooking apples to make this excellent jelly, to be served with hot or cold meats.

4 lb (1.8 kg) cooking apples   12 sprigs or more fresh basil
2 pints (1.1 litres) water   4 tbsp lemon juice
unrefined granulated sugar

Wipe the apples and chop them roughly. Since the pulp will eventually be strained, it is not necessary to peel or core them. Put them in a saucepan with the water, bring to the boil and simmer until really soft, stirring occasionally and pressing the fruit against the side of the pan. Remove the pulp to a jelly bag, suspended above a large bowl, and leave to drip through overnight.

The next day, pour the juice into a measuring jug, before transferring it to a pan. Add 1 lb (450 g) sugar for every pint of jelly, along with the basil sprigs and lemon juice. Boil until setting point is reached, remove the basil and pour into jars before sealing and storing in the usual way (see Jams and Jellies).

Aubergines

Aubergines are now a common sight in British greengrocers, imported largely from Spain and Italy, although they originated in Asia. They are at their cheapest and best in the autumn, when they combine well with dishes containing courgettes or sweet peppers. You will also often come across them being sold off cheaply if they are past their best, and although a very wrinkled or dull skin indicates excessive age, there is nothing wrong with snapping up a few pounds of just slightly damaged ones. You will need to use them quickly though, so try the recipes below for an interesting variety of dishes.

Aubergines can be any shape from quite small and round (hence the name used in America, 'eggplant') to long and oval. The colour varies from dark black-purple to pale mauve, the former being the most common here. The slightly earthy taste is remarkably consistent, regardless of size. The flesh should be firm, even if the skin is damaged, as any softness suggests bruised or rotten flesh under the skin.

It is rarely necessary nowadays to salt the slices and leave them to drain out the bitter juices, since modern breeds are milder. On the other hand salting does cut down on the amount of oil the spongy flesh soaks up if you are frying them. (Slice, score with a knife, sprinkle with salt and leave for 30 minutes in a colander before rinsing well.). Whether you peel them or not is a matter for personal taste – I find it unnecessary, but some complain the skin is rather tough.

Poor Man's Caviar

This excellent aubergine dip often goes by the name poor man's caviar, although it bears no resemblance to the real thing. However, aubergines are highly esteemed all over the Middle East and this certainly brings out the best in them. The version here is quite pungent, reduce the amount of garlic if you're serving it for lunch and don't want to be ostracized in the afternoon.

Serves 6

2 large aubergines (about
   1½ lb/670 g)
½ medium onion
1 large clove garlic
2 tbsp olive oil

2 tbsp lemon juice
pinch paprika
seasoning
1 tbsp fresh chopped parsley or
   mint

Wipe the aubergines and prick them all over with a fork. Bake them on a tray in an oven set to Gas 6/400°F/200°C, for 45 minutes until soft. Cool slightly and cut in half lengthways, then scoop out the soft flesh with a spoon. Finely chop the onion and garlic, before beating in the aubergine flesh, oil, lemon juice, paprika and seasoning. (You can do this in a food processor if you have one.) Pile into a bowl and sprinkle with the fresh mint or parsley.

Serve with warm pitta bread or crudités (raw vegetables cut into batons) as an appetizing starter or a dip with pre-dinner drinks.

Aubergine and Yoghurt Salad

If you're having a slightly spicy main course, this makes a good alternative to the Mint and Cucumber Yoghurt Salad on page 43. If you can get hold of some Greek cow's yoghurt, it has a less sharp, creamier taste.

Serves 4

2 small aubergines
2 tbsp wholemeal flour
2 heaped tsp ground cumin
sunflower oil for frying
small tub (150 g) natural yoghurt

squeeze lemon juice
1 tbsp fresh chopped mint or
   1 level tsp dried
black pepper

Halve the aubergines and slice them quite thickly, then toss them in the flour and ground cumin, which you have mixed together in a shallow bowl. Heat approximately ½ inch (1 cm) of oil in a frying pan and fry the aubergines in about four batches until golden brown, turning once. Drain well on kitchen paper.

Beat the yoghurt with the lemon juice until it is smooth and not too solid. Stir in the mint and black pepper and coat the aubergine slices, mixing well. Turn into a serving bowl and chill.

Veronese Aubergine Gratin

This recipe is adapted from one given to me by Giovanni Centomo, the chef at the Ristorante Nuovo Marconi in Verona, Italy, a restaurant popular with heads of state as well as locals. There it is served as a first course but it would make a good supper dish for two as well.

Fresh basil leaves are important as dried basil gives a bitter taste in this dish. I have tried it with bottled pesto instead, which is quite good, but does make the finished dish a bit oily – you need to mop the edges before serving.

Serves 4 as a starter

1 large aubergine	black pepper
6 ripe medium tomatoes	6 oz (170 g) Mozzarella cheese
1 tsp tomato purée	4 tbsp grated Parmesan cheese
½ clove garlic	bunch fresh basil
small pinch salt	sunflower or olive oil for frying

Peel the aubergine and cut it lengthways into 8 medium-thick slices. Liquidize the tomatoes or chop them, push through a sieve to remove the pips and pour off a little of the excess liquid, before mixing with the tomato purée, crushed garlic and seasoning.

Slice the Mozzarella thinly and roughly chop the basil leaves. Heat some oil in a frying pan and fry the aubergine slices until golden brown. If you need to add more oil, make sure it's really hot before putting in the aubergines, or they will absorb too much and become rather soggy. Drain on kitchen paper.

Spread half the tomato mixture over the bottom of an oval gratin dish and cover with 4 of the aubergine slices. Sprinkle with some basil and both sorts of cheese. Repeat the layers, ending with cheese. Bake in an oven pre-heated to Gas 7/425°F/220°F for 15-20 minutes until the top is golden brown and bubbling.

Ratatouille

This classic Provençal dish is delicious hot or cold and comparatively cheap to make in the early autumn, when the principal ingredients are in season. Don't overcook it or it will become a mush – all the vegetables should be recognizable both in appearance and flavour.

Serves 4-6

2 medium aubergines	2 medium courgettes
2 medium onions	2 large cloves garlic
4 medium tomatoes	1 tsp ground coriander
1 medium red pepper	seasoning
1 medium green pepper	oil for frying

Cut the aubergines into bite-sized chunks, halve and slice the onions. Peel the tomatoes, scalding them first in boiling water to loosen the skins, and chop them roughly. Deseed and slice the red and green peppers, slice the courgettes quite thickly.

Fry the aubergine pieces in hot olive or sunflower oil until lightly browned – if you deep-fry them they will use up less oil and take less time. Drain well.

Heat 3 tablespoons of olive oil in a large frying pan and fry the onions with the crushed garlic. As they start to soften add the peppers, then the aubergines and courgettes, stirring occasionally. Cover and simmer gently for 25 minutes.

Sprinkle the vegetables with the coriander and seasoning and stir in the chopped tomatoes. Cook for a further 10 minutes, uncovered. If the oil has not all been absorbed by now you may like to drain it off.

Spicy Aubergines

This makes an excellent accompaniment to an Indian curry such as the Lamb Gosht Maurya on page 33, or it could be served with rice as a vegetarian meal. The quantities given here are suitable to feed six as a side dish.

Serves 6

2 medium aubergines	1½ tsp ground coriander
3 medium tomatoes	1½ tsp ground cumin
1 medium onion	2 bayleaves
1 large clove garlic	few tbsp water
6 tbsp sunflower oil	black pepper
1 level tsp chilli powder	

Remove the stems from the aubergines and slice them in half, then cut into cubes about 1½ inches (2 cm) square. Peel the tomatoes by dropping them into boiling water for the count of 10, then into cold – this loosens the skin. Quarter them and then slice the onion.

Heat the oil in a frying pan and cook the onion for a few minutes with the crushed garlic. Turn the heat up and fry the aubergine until beginning to change colour (about 5 minutes), then add the tomatoes, spices and bayleaves. Stir well, adding a little water if all the oil has been absorbed by the aubergines. Cover and simmer 15-20 minutes, stirring occasionally. Season with black pepper and serve.

Stuffed Aubergines

Those not used to cooking for vegetarians may lack inspiration when it comes to mealtime entertaining. These stuffed aubergines are a tasty as well as nutritious main course and, even better, they freeze well, which means you can whip one out of the freezer should a supper guest not warn you in advance that they don't eat meat.

Serves 4

2 large aubergines	1 tsp tomato purée
1 large onion	pinch dried thyme
2 oz (55 g) mushrooms	pinch dried marjoram
4 medium tomatoes	1 tbsp fresh chopped parsley
1 clove garlic	2 tbsp cooked brown rice
1-2 tbsp olive oil	2 tbsp chopped pine or other nuts

Halve the aubergines lengthways and scoop out enough of the flesh in the centre to fit in the stuffing. Set the scooped-out flesh on one side. Chop the onion and mushrooms, deseed and chop 2 of the tomatoes. Soften the onion and crushed garlic in the oil, then add the mushrooms, scooped-out aubergine flesh, chopped tomatoes, tomato purée and herbs. Simmer gently for 5 minutes, season and add the rice and pine nuts.

Fill the aubergines with the mixture. Slice the remaining tomatoes and arrange on top of the aubergines, then bake wrapped in silver foil for 1 hour at Gas 3/325°F/170°C.

Moussaka

This classic Greek dish can be much abused, even in Greece, where I have experienced very oily versions. It is also common in Greece to serve the dish lukewarm, whereas in our colder climate it is better eaten served hot. A trick to avoid the aubergines' soaking up too much oil is to deep-fry the slices at a much higher temperature – this produces quicker browning with less oil wastage. Ideally you should use olive oil, but this can be expensive when used in quantity, so sunflower can be substituted, although the flavour will of course be slightly different. You can make moussaka with minced chicken, for a lighter-flavoured dish.

Serves 4

3 medium aubergines
olive or sunflower oil for frying
3 medium onions
1¼ lb (550 g) minced lamb
2 cloves garlic
1 tsp ground cinnamon
3 tbsp fresh chopped parsley

seasoning
7½ fl. oz (225 ml) lamb or chicken
  stock
1 dsp tomato purée
½ pint (300 ml) béchamel sauce
  (see page 178)
4 tbsp grated Parmesan cheese

Slice the aubergines fairly thickly into rounds of just over ½ inch (1.5 cm). Fry them in the oil until lightly browned and soft, using the deep-fry method if you wish. Remove and set aside. Chop the onions and colour them in the oil (adding more if required), then add the lamb and crushed garlic and stir until the meat has browned, before mixing in the cinnamon and parsley.

Take an ovenproof dish and cover the bottom with aubergine slices. Spread on some of the meat mixture, season and repeat, finishing with a layer of aubergine. Heat the stock and tomato purée together, pour into the dish at the side and cook in an oven preheated to Gas 3/325°F/170°C for 45 minutes or until the stock is almost absorbed. Meanwhile make the béchamel sauce in the usual way.

Add most of the Parmesan cheese to the sauce and pour over the aubergine and mince. Sprinkle with the remaining cheese and turn up the oven so the dish browns at Gas 5/375°F/190°C for about 20 minutes. Get rid of any excess oil by spooning it off or mopping it up with kitchen paper before serving with a crisp green salad.

Blackberries

Of all the hedgerow fruits available for the picking, blackberries are the best known and most plentiful. They have been gathered from the wild for thousands of years, and although now they are grown for commercial sale the cultivated ones are in no way superior to the wild, so if you are able it makes sense to harvest them for free.

It is quite common to come across an unexpected crop while out walking. After picking them into whatever container or bag you might have to hand, you return home triumphantly only to be faced with the problem of what to do with them before they go bad. Any that are overripe will deteriorate even more quickly than usual (you should cook, eat and preserve them very soon after picking, for by the next day they

will already be going mushy). The need for speed means you have to
have a good range of recipes up your sleeve if you are to take the best
advantage of the annual crop without ever getting bored.

When picking blackberries avoid busy roadsides and any verges that
look as if they may have been sprayed with insecticide. Don't pick the
very small blackberries which will be full of seeds. It also advisable to
wear jeans, shoes and long-sleeved shirts - not a sweater or you will get
hooked up in the thorns !

See also the blackberry sauce to accompany Poached Peaches.

Blackberry Soup

This makes an unusual first course at an autumn dinner, served hot or
chilled. It is now becoming increasingly common to serve fruit as a
first course in some form – after all we've been eating melon as a starter
for years.

Serves 4

1 lb (450 g) blackberries
1½ pints (850 ml) water
bayleaf
2 inch (5cm) stick cinnamon
6 cloves
few blades mace

few black peppercorns
1 tbsp clear honey
3 tbsp port
4 tsp arrowroot
2 tbsp cold water
¼ pint (150 ml) single cream

Wash the blackberries briefly in a colander under cold water and throw
out any that are a bit rotten. Put the rest into a pan with the water,
bayleaf, spices and honey, bring to the boil stirring occasionally and
simmer for 10 minutes. Sieve and return to the pan with the port, heat
gently for a few minutes then stir in the cream and the arrowroot,
dissolved in a couple of tablespoons of cold water. Continue stirring until
the soup thickens then serve or chill.

Poached Pears with Blackberry Sauce

You can eat this excellent dessert hot or cold. Make sure you include the
spices listed for a truly mulled flavour to the sauce. Choose pears that are
ripe without being too soft as you don't want them to disintegrate during
cooking.

Serves 4

8 oz (225 g) blackberries
4 good-sized pears
½ pint (300 ml) red wine
½ pint (300 ml) water
½ tsp ground cinnamon

2 strips orange peel
squeeze lemon juice
3 cloves
1 tbsp clear honey (optional)

Halve the pears, scoop out the core and then peel them. Lay them in one layer in an ovenproof dish. Mix the wine with the water and pour it all over the dish, then cover with silver foil. Bake in an oven preheated to Gas 4/350°F/180°C for 45 minutes.

Remove the pears and keep them warm if you are serving the dish hot. (Pouring the hot sauce over them at the end will heat them up fairly effectively if they are just gently warm.) Boil the red wine fast until it has reduced in volume by nearly one half, then add the blackberries, which you have washed briefly, and all the other ingredients except the honey. Simmer gently for 5-10 minutes, then sieve, reheat and taste. You may want to add a little honey for sweetening at this stage, in which case you should stir the sauce until the honey has dissolved. Pour the sauce over the pears and serve.

If you are serving the dish cold, allow the sauce to cool before pouring it over the fruit.

Blackberry and Apple Pasty

We are all familiar with the traditional Cornish pasty, filled with potato and chopped meat. Here is a sweet version, made with puff pastry for a lighter effect and stuffed with delicious blackberry and apple.

Makes 6

12 oz (335 g) blackberries
13 oz (430 g) packet puff pastry
1 cooking apple

2 tbsp dried wholemeal
  breadcrumbs
3 tsp clear honey
beaten egg

Cut the pastry into 6 pieces and roll them out individually on a floured surface. Cut out 6 circles using a 6 inch (15 cm) diameter plate as a guide. Put these in the fridge to chill.

Peel, quarter and core the apple. Slice it thinly and cut each slice in half. Wash the blackberries briefly and pat really dry on kitchen paper. Preheat the oven to Gas 7/425°F/220°C.

Take each pastry circle and place a few slices of apple down the centre. Sprinkle with a few breadcrumbs, pile some blackberries on top, add half a teaspoon of honey (at the most) and sprinkle with some more breadcrumbs (these will absorb the juice as the pasty cooks and help prevent it leaking through). Brush the edges of the pastry with water and join the two sides at the top, pinching the join together well with your fingers.

Place the pasties on a wet baking tray, brush the surfaces with beaten egg and bake for 15-20 minutes until the pastry is golden brown. Serve hot or cold.

Bramble Jelly

The very name of this delicious jelly brings back memories for me of long days blackberrying by our local river, the Medway in Kent, when early autumn always seemed to turn out as an Indian summer. Blackberrying is a peculiarly British sport but over the past ten years it seems to have been dying out – it is much simpler to find the good plump juicy berries now than it was previously, when you had to clamber right into the bush to pick those that others thought were out of reach.

When making jelly with blackberries, you need to add extra acid to bring out the little pectin they have, or they won't set. It is a good idea to include a few unripe berries, as this also helps the setting. Don't expect the end-result to be anything like as firm as a red- or blackcurrant jelly, however.

This is lovely served on scones or bread for tea.

4 lb (1.8 kg) blackberries   1 pint water
2 lemons   unrefined granulated sugar

Wash the fruit very briefly in a colander under a gentle stream of cold water. Peel the lemons and squeeze the juice from them, then tie the skin and pips in a little muslin bag to provide extra acidity. Put the blackberries into a large pan with the water and lemon juice. Tie the muslin bag to the saucepan handle and immerse it in the fruit. Simmer until completely soft (about 25 minutes), then leave to strain overnight through a jelly bag.

Measure the juice and pour it into a large pan with 1 lb (450 g) sugar to every pint (550 ml) of liquid. Stir gently over a low heat until the sugar has completely dissolved, then boil rapidly until setting point is reached (a thermometer is particularly useful here, as otherwise you may start to dither about whether it's going to set any stiffer and miss the moment altogether).

Pour into warm jampots, cover in the usual way (see Jams and Jellies) and leave to grow cold before labelling and storing in a cool dry place.

Blackberry and Apple Jam

Apples, which are rich in pectin and acid, are often added to blackberries when making jam to help it set. I add the juice of a lemon as well just to be sure. Those who can't bear blackberry pips should follow Method 2, although I find them so small as not to be really bothersome.

Makes about 7 lb (3 kg)
3 lb (1.35 kg) blackberries
1¼ lb (550 g) cooking apples
juice of 1 lemon

2 tbsp water
3½ lb (1.55 kg) unrefined
    granulated sugar

Method 1

Wash the blackberries briefly in a colander under gently running cold water. Peel, core and chop the apples. Put both fruit into a pan with the water and lemon juice and simmer until soft, about 25 minutes. Stir in the sugar over a gentle heat until it has completely dissolved then boil rapidly until setting point is reached. Pot and cover in the usual way (see Jams and Jellies) before labelling and storing in a cool dry place.

Method 2

Wash the blackberries as above, then simmer them with the lemon juice until soft. Rub them through a sieve. Simmer the chopped apples in the water until really soft, add the blackberry pulp and the warmed sugar. Proceed as above.

Blackberry Vinegar Drink

This an old recipe from Boscastle in Cornwall. You may think it slightly odd to have vinegar as the base for a drink, but once mixed with the blackberry juices and afterwards diluted with water, it is rather refreshing. The sharpness of the vinegar is tempered by the honey.

3 lbs (1.35 kg) blackberries
1 pint (550 ml) wine vinegar
clear honey to taste (about 6tbsp)

12 cloves
2 oz (55 g) root ginger

Pour the vinegar over the blackberries and leave in a bowl to soak for 24 hours. Strain, pushing through as much juice as you can and add the honey to taste, cloves and peeled ginger. Simmer for 30 minutes, strain and bottle, sealing the bottles with corks, cut to fit if necessary.

    To drink, stir 1-2 tablespoons of blackberry vinegar into a glass of iced still or soda water.

Celery

Traditionally celery is an autumn and winter vegetable, carefully 'earthed up' in trenches to improve the flavour and keep the stems white. However, modern times have seen the development of the self-blanching varieties, which if grown here have to be dug up before the frosts arrive, but which are also imported, particularly from Spain. From the gastronomic point of view, the traditional type is by far the tastiest, and although rather more stringy, the texture is crisper too.

Celery does not keep as long as one expects. The stalks become limp and wilted after just a few days, and although it is always a good idea to have a head of celery in the fridge to use in salads, stocks and so on, you may find from time to time that you have a surplus that has to be consumed quickly.

Celery is a versatile vegetable, being equally good in salads, in soups, stir-fried or gently braised. Plainly boiled I find it rather slimy, but added to stocks and casseroles it imparts a delicious flavour. Choose heads that are firm and tightly packed, with fresh-looking upright leaves at the top. The 'green' varieties do not need much washing, but the English white sort often still has quantities of earth clinging to it, and needs to have the stems individually scrubbed after trimming off the root and top (keep these for flavouring stock).

Celery Boats with Stilton

Celery stalks are useful 'containers' when preparing food for drinks parties. Apart from slicing the stalks into 3 inch (7.5 cm) lengths and then splitting these into two or three pieces to surround a Guacamole dip (see page 146) along with other crudités such as raw carrots, green and red peppers, cauliflower florets and button mushrooms speared on cocktail sticks, they make good 'boats' for filling with hummus, taramasalata, garlicky cream cheese or softened Stilton.

Makes 30-40
1 head crisp celery
8 oz (225 g) Stilton cheese

a little milk
2 oz (55 g) finely chopped nuts

Trim the celery stalks and scrub them with a nail brush, then divide each into 3 or 4 lengths, about 2 inches (5 cm) long. Mash the Stilton well with a fork and beat in the milk until you have a smooth and fairly soft purée (a food processor makes light work of this). Spoon the mixture into a piping bag fitted with a starred nozzle and pipe it into each boat. Roll the surface gently in the chopped nuts, shortly before serving. (If you do it too far ahead the nuts will go soggy.)

Alternatively use low-fat soft cheese mixed with a crushed clove of garlic. You can also fill the celery with hummus or taramasalata, in which case you should sprinkle the tops with fresh chopped parsley or mint rather than nuts.

Celery and Stilton Soup

This is a real autumnal soup, heralding the approach of Christmas. There is no point in making it with the rather insipid, green imported celery – you need the home-grown variety, the whiter the better for a stronger flavour. When making this soup it is fine to use the outer stalks of your celery head, keeping the tender heart for salads or braising.

Serves 4

1 head celery	1½ pints (850 ml) chicken stock
1 medium onion	2 oz (55 g) Stilton cheese
1 tbsp sunflower oil	seasoning
½ oz (15 g) butter	

Trim the base from the celery and scrub the stalks well to remove any earth. Return the heart to the bottom of the fridge and slice the outer stalks thickly. Slice the onion. Heat the oil and butter in a thick-bottomed pan and sweat the sliced vegetables, covered, for about 10 minutes. Add the chicken stock and simmer, covered, for 20 minutes, then liquidize.

Grate the Stilton (you'll find it will crumble into bits as well, the main thing is to make sure the pieces are really small). Stir it into the soup, over the heat, until it is completely melted. Taste for seasoning – I find it needs very little, as the two main flavours are already quite strong.

Celery, Grapefruit and Nut salad

This is an excellent combination of contrasting textures, and the flavour is further enhanced by the warm sesame seed dressing. It is also one of the few salads that keep well – you can eat any leftovers the next day. If you can't find cashew nuts (sold unsalted in many wholefood shops) use chopped unblanched hazelnuts.

Serves 4

½ head celery	black pepper
1 pink grapefruit	2 tbsp olive oil
2 oz (55 g) unsalted cashew nuts	1 tbsp sesame seeds
½ tbsp fresh chopped tarragon	

Halve the grapefruit and remove the segments, keeping any juice and squeezing it out of the shells into a small bowl. Scrub the celery and slice it. Chop the cashew nuts finely. Mix all these in a salad bowl with the tarragon. Add some freshly ground black pepper.

Heat the oil in a small saucepan and fry the sesame seeds until golden brown. Add the reserved grapefruit juice and when it is sizzling hot pour the sauce over the salad. Serve immediately.

Braised Celery

A traditional way of cooking that has been rather neglected of late, braising brings out the best flavour in celery. The important thing is not to overcook it, or it goes rather slimy. Also make sure the heat is kept low, as the stock should be just simmering, not boiling. You can use the stock afterwards to make a delicious soup base.

Use only the hearts of the celery heads, the outer stalks are generally rather stringy and should be kept for making soup or a stock. Some supermarkets now sell celery hearts already prepared.

Serves 4

4 hearts celery
4 oz (110 g) unsmoked bacon
1 medium onion
6-8 oz (170-225 g) carrots

1 oz (30 g) butter
1-1½ pints (550-850 ml) chicken
   stock
seasoning

If you are dealing with whole celery heads, cut off the tops to leave the main part about 5 inches (13 cm) long. Strip off the outer stalks. Derind and dice the bacon, slice the onion and carrots. Bring a large pan of water to the boil and drop the celery hearts in for 10 minutes.

Meanwhile sauté the onion, carrots and bacon in the butter in a small flameproof casserole for 5 minutes. Add the drained celery hearts and pour over enough stock to almost cover them. Bring to the boil, season lightly and lower the heat so the liquid is just simmering. Cover and leave for 30-35 minutes until tender when pierced with a fork. Lift out and serve.

Creamy Celery with Almonds

The occasional use of cream does make a simple vegetable dish something special. This goes very well with plainly roasted pork or beef, and the crunchiness of the almonds adds an interesting texture.

Serves 4

1 large head celery	1-2 dsp wholemeal flour
3 oz (85 g) blanched almonds	2½ fl. oz (75 ml) chicken stock
¼ medium onion	up to ¼ pint (150 ml) single cream
1 oz (30 g) butter	seasoning
small pinch caraway seeds	

Trim and wash the celery well and cut it into 2 inch (5 cm) lengths.
Bring some water to the boil and simmer the celery for about 5 minutes,
then drain. Spread the almonds on a tray and brown in an oven set to
about Gas 4/350°F/180°C, taking care they don't burn. Once they have
turned golden brown, cool them and cut into slivers.

Slice the onion and sweat it with the celery and caraway seeds in the
butter in a thick-bottomed casserole, with a close-fitting lid, over a very
low heat for 15 minutes. Check occasionally to make sure the vegetables
aren't sticking, in which case add a little stock. After this time stir in the
flour to absorb the fat and add the stock and cream slowly, stirring well
until you have a smooth sauce. Season if necessary, stir in the almonds
and serve.

Chestnuts with Celery Sauce

This is an excellent way of using up the end part of a head of celery,
when the rest has already gone into a salad or a soup. The sauce is based
on the classic béchamel, which has dozens of different uses in vegetable
cookery. You should use the traditionally grown English celery, if
possible, rather than the imported self-blanching kind.

Serves 4

⅓ celery head	½ oz (15 g) butter
2 lb (900 g) chestnuts	seasoning
1 pint (550 ml) good stock	1 tbsp fresh chopped parsley
½ pint (300 ml) béchamel sauce	
(see page 178)	

To peel the chestnuts, put them into boiling water in small batches and
simmer for 5 minutes. Lift them out with a slotted spoon and remove the
tough outer and thin inner skin with a small knife while they are still
hot. Once they start to cool they become more difficult to peel, in which
case return them to the boiling water. It is easiest to do this wearing
rubber gloves, so you can handle them while really hot, with the next
batch already boiling.

Put the chestnuts in a covered saucepan with the stock to simmer for
20 minutes until tender. Don't let them get too soft. Meanwhile make
the béchamel sauce in the usual way. Next, take a piece of celery, trim

off the root and chop the celery finely. Sweat in a little butter until really soft. Mix into the béchamel (you may want to sieve the celery first if it is rather stringy). Test for seasoning.

Drain the chestnuts, leaving them whole (keep the stock for a soup). Put them into a hot serving dish and pour the celery sauce all over. Sprinkle with a little chopped parsley and serve with roast chicken or turkey.

Mushrooms

It is often possible to find mushrooms at up to half the normal price, especially in markets. These are ones that are just past their best, or broken up and therefore considered not prime quality. So long as they have not turned brownish, or acquired a slightly slimy sheen on the top, by all means snap them up. But how many times, you may be saying, have you done this, only to run out of original ways to serve them and have them rot at the bottom of the fridge? The recipes below should solve that problem, with enough suggestions not only to help you use up cut-price mushrooms past their peak, but also to encourage you to seek out top quality ones – or even the wild variety.

Fungi have been gathered wild for thousands of years, and the number of different edible species is staggering. While in many European countries mushroom-gathering is a national pastime if not an obsession, here in Britain we regard anything other than the field mushroom (which in its more immature stages is sold as the button mushroom) with suspicion. This is not the place to go into the delights of wild mushrooms, suffice it to say that once you are converted, you too will be up at four in the morning scouring the woods and fields.

The mushrooms that are on sale in our shops are all grown commerically in dark sheds or cellars and so are available throughout the year. However, I have included them in the autumn section of this book, since this is their true season in the wild.

Choose ones with firm white skins and clean gills (the larger the better, the button ones really don't have much flavour, although the texture is pleasant when you eat them raw). It is not necessary to peel them, simply wipe the top with a clean damp cloth. The stalks have as much if not more flavour than the rest and should not be discarded.

See also Pork Fillet with Apple and Mushrooms.

Iced Mushroom and Prawn Soup

This soup looks very dark and thick until the cream is stirred in, but the bread does give a good texture. Use the big flat mushrooms with dark gills, if you can, for extra flavour. Should you wish to use a stock cube instead of the homemade chicken stock, make it up under strength or it will dominate the taste of the soup.

Serves 4

12 oz (335 g) mushrooms
4 oz (110 g) unshelled prawns
2 slices wholemeal bread
small clove garlic
2 tbsp sunflower oil
1 pint (550 ml) homemade
    chicken stock
seasoning

2½ fl. oz (75ml) single cream

Stock
prawn shells
¼ medium onion
¾ pint (425 ml) water
bayleaf
black peppercorns

Peel the prawns and boil up the shells with the other stock ingredients for 15 minutes, covered. Wipe the mushrooms and chop finely, using a food processor if you wish. Remove the crusts from the bread and break it into chunks.

Cook the mushrooms in the oil with the crushed garlic and bread over a low heat with the lid on until the mushrooms start to produce liquid. Strain the prawn stock and add it with the chicken stock to the mushrooms, season quite well and simmer, covered, for 10-15 minutes. Liquidize and chill.

Chop the prawns and keep them in the fridge with the cream until shortly before you sit down to eat, then stir both in and serve.

Mushroom and Rice Soup

If you have any pheasant stock available, it makes an excellent and tasty base for this soup, otherwise chicken stock may be used. This is quite a thick hearty soup, very suitable for the chill of the first autumn nights. It is necessary to use the larger mushrooms with brown gills to provide the colour.

Serves 4

8 oz (225 g) mushrooms
1 medium onion
1 clove garlic
1 tbsp sunflower oil
1 tbsp wholemeal flour
1½ pints (850 ml) chicken stock

1½ oz (45 g) easy cook brown rice
bayleaf
½ pint (300 ml) milk
seasoning
3 tbsp fresh chopped parsley

Wipe the mushrooms and chop them really finely (a food processor is ideal). Finely chop the onion and sauté it in the oil with the crushed garlic for about 3 minutes. Add the mushrooms, lower the heat and cook for a further 5-7 minutes. Stir in the wholemeal flour and cook another minute before pouring in the stock with the rice. Add the bayleaf, bring to the boil and simmer, covered, for 20-25 minutes.

Pour in the milk, remove the bayleaf and reheat gently. Test for seasoning and serve sprinkled with the chopped parsley.

If you are using ordinary brown rice, which takes 40-45 minutes to cook, simmer it first for about 20 minutes in water before adding to the soup as above.

Mushrooms à la Grecque

This is an excellent side dish or starter to make when you see button mushrooms on sale at reduced prices, since any slight damage is not noticeable after they have been simmered in the sauce. The reduction of the sauce by nearly half concentrates the flavours of the wine and tomato.

Serves 4

1 lb (450 g) small button
   mushrooms
½ medium onion
1 clove garlic
2 tbsp olive oil
2 tbsp tomato purée
4 tbsp dry white wine

½ tsp coriander seeds
pinch thyme
squeeze lemon juice
seasoning
¾ pint (425 ml) water
1 tbsp fresh chopped parsley

Finely chop the onion and cook it gently in the oil with the crushed garlic for a few minutes until soft, but not browned. Stir in the tomato purée, then the wine and add all the other ingredients except the mushrooms. Bring to the boil and simmer for 10-15 minutes.

Meanwhile wipe the mushrooms with a clean damp cloth. After the initial cooking time has elapsed, add the mushrooms to the dish and cook gently for a further 10 minutes. Lift the mushrooms out with a slotted spoon and set to one side, then turn up the heat and boil the sauce until it has reduced by almost half.

To serve hot, return the mushrooms to the pan to coat them well in the sauce and heat through, before transferring to individual dishes and sprinkling with the parsley. They are equally good cold (though not chilled), in which case put the mushrooms in a shallow dish and pour the sauce over. Sprinkle with the parsley and leave to cool.

Stuffed Mushrooms

I prefer to use one large flat mushroom per person for this dish, since they are much tastier than lots of little button ones (and quicker to prepare). They can be got ready in advance and just popped under the grill at the last moment to reheat. You can serve them either as an accompanying vegetable to a plain fish or meat course, or as a starter.

Serves 4

4 large mushrooms (total weight
   8-12 oz/225-335 g)
½ medium onion
1 clove garlic
1 oz (30 g) butter
pinch dried thyme

1 tsp ground cumin
1 tbsp chopped walnuts
1 tbsp fresh chopped parsley
1 medium tomato
black pepper
little olive oil

Wipe the outsides of the mushrooms and pluck out the centre stalks carefully. Chop these, and finely chop the onion, then cook together with the crushed garlic in the butter and thyme until slightly soft. Stir in the cumin, nuts and parsley. Pile on to the mushroom shells and top with a slice of tomato. Sprinkle with freshly ground black pepper and dribble a little olive oil over. Wrap each mushroom in an envelope of silver foil and bake on a tray at Gas 6/400°F/200°C for 30 minutes.

Lift out of the juices and serve.

Mushroom and Chestnut Stuffing

Why not make this in advance for Christmas and freeze it ? The quantities are suitable for stuffing a 10-12 lb (4.5-5.5 kg) turkey.

6 oz (170 g) mushrooms
1½ lb (670 g) chestnuts
¾ pint (425 ml) milk or stock
1 small onion
2 oz (55 g) butter

1 oz (30 g) fresh wholemeal
   breadcrumbs
1 heaped tbsp fresh chopped
   parsley
1 beaten egg
seasoning

Peel the chestnuts (see Chestnuts with Celery Sauce, page 120) then cook them in the stock or milk for 20-30 minutes until tender. Strain, keeping the cooking liquor to one side, and purée in a food processor or sieve them. Meanwhile finely chop the onion and cook it in the butter over a low heat.

Chop the mushrooms and add them to the onion, cover and cook gently, shaking occasionally, until the mushrooms have given off quite a bit of juice. Drain well and mix with the chestnuts and all the other ingredients, including a good pinch of salt and lots of black pepper. You will probably need to use a little of the liquid the chestnuts have cooked in to form a smooth purée, but don't make it too sloppy.

For using later, pack it into a rigid container and freeze. Fill the breast of the bird with the stuffing and sew the flap down with button thread to prevent the stuffing from oozing out during cooking.

The chestnut-flavoured milk or stock can be used to form the base of an excellent soup.

Pickled Mushrooms

This pickle doesn't keep for more than about six weeks, so make it in small batches using the quantities below, and use up fairly quickly. Choose little, firm button mushrooms, either those which are completely closed up, or ones with very fine pale gills.

Makes 1 medium Kilner jar

1 lb (450 g) button mushrooms
just over ¼ pt (150 ml) white wine
   vinegar
1 inch (2.5 cm) stick cinnamon
2-3 blades mace

3 slices fresh ginger
1 tsp black peppercorns
6 cloves
1 sprig fresh or a small pinch dried
   tarragon

Put the vinegar, spices and tarragon into a saucepan with a close-fitting lid, bring to the boil and simmer for 15 minutes.

In the meantime wash the mushrooms in a colander under cold running water, rubbing off any clinging earth. Put them into a saucepan and pour on the pickling vinegar through a strainer. Bring to the boil and simmer gently till the mushrooms are just tender and have shrunk somewhat (about 7 minutes), stirring occasionally.

Lift out the mushrooms into a clean jar. Cool the vinegar for 10 minutes or so and pour over while still warm. Seal, label and store for 2 weeks before using. Eat within 6-8 weeks.

Mushroom Ketchup

This used to be a staple ingredient of any storecupboard, before the food industry developed a hundred and one ways to spice up your soups, gravies and stews with a bewildering array of powders, crystals and liquids, most containing an offputting range of additives and 'added flavourings' drawn from who knows where. Homemade mushroom ketchup adds a real zest to winter casseroles or rather bland soups, in the same way that soy sauce can pep up the dullest of Chinese vegetable platters. It is also an excellent way of using a real abundance of cheap mushrooms.

There are two schools of thought regarding this traditional ketchup. The first adds considerable quantities of vinegar, which limits the sauce's use to dishes which can cope with this strong flavour. The other uses none at all, which means the end-result is more versatile, but also more expensive to make. I have chosen a middle road, and added a small amount of vinegar, which adds spice to the ketchup without overwhelming it. In either case you should make this when there is a real glut of the flat mushrooms with dark brown gills, to keep the cost economical.

Makes about 1 pint

2 lb (900 g) flat dark mushrooms	1-2 tbsp brandy
2½ oz (70 g) salt	1 inch (2.5 cm) piece fresh ginger
up to ¼ pint (150 ml) wine	few blades mace
vinegar	few black peppercorns

Wipe the tops of the mushrooms to remove any dirt, then break them up into chunks. Put them into a lidded glass or china ovenproof dish, interspersing the layers with a good sprinkling of the salt. Cover and leave for up to 3 days in a fairly cool place, turning occasionally and pressing against the side of the dish with a large spoon. The juice will gradually be drawn out of the mushrooms.

After this time put the dish in the oven at Gas 3/325°F/170°C for an hour. Remove and strain the contents through a sieve, pressing hard to extract the maximum amount of juice. Discard the mushrooms. Measure the juice and add ¼ pint (150 ml) of wine vinegar and 2 tablespoons of brandy to every pint (550 ml) of liquid. Pour this into a saucepan, peel the ginger and add it with the other spices then simmer gently, covered, for 15 minutes.

Strain into small clean Kilner jars while still hot, and seal. Sterilize by simmering the jars upright in a pan of water for 20 minutes. This is very important as it prevents the ketchup from fermenting. Use sparingly and remember the ketchup contains quite a bit of salt, so you don't need to add any more to the dishes you use it in.

Pheasant

Pheasant is one of the best-known and cheaper game birds, introduced from the Far East some hundreds of years ago. Its flesh contains much less fat than red meats, partly because for at least some of its life it is wild and must forage for its own food, which gives a leaner texture to the meat. With the current awareness in Britain of the need for a healthier diet, including a reduction in the amount of fat we eat, game is rapidly becoming more popular. It can now even be found, in season, in chain supermarkets as well as the traditional game dealers.

The season for pheasant is 1st October to 31st January and true game aficionados frown on eating it after that, even though it has been shot legally in season and kept in the freezer. This fairly short period means that it is best to serve pheasant in a variety of ways in order not to jade the palate. Apart from offering you a range of ideas, the recipes here also provide ways of cooking pheasant for those who find its gamey flavour too strong if the bird is simply roasted.

Pheasants are sold either singly or as a brace, which consists of a hen (female) and cock (male). The hen is smaller, serving only two to three people, but tastier, while the larger cock can stretch to four if cooked cleverly. It is essential for the bird to be hung after being killed, in order to develop the flavour. This is done by suspending it with string from the neck in a cool airy place for anything between four days and three weeks, depending on the temperature and your personal taste. The longer it is hung, the stronger the gamey flavour. The bird should not be plucked until after it has been hung, and is ready to be eaten when the tail feathers pull out easily. A badly shot bird cannot be hung as long as a cleanly killed one. For roasting choose young pheasant – the beak should be pliable and the feet soft, not scaly as in older birds, which are more suitable for casseroling or making into pâtés.

When you buy pheasant from a poulterer's (often combined with a traditional fishmonger's) or butcher's, they will pluck and draw it for you. For those people who may be presented with one as a gift here is how to cope.

To pluck   Hold the pheasant firmly head down over a large sheet of newspaper or a plastic rubbish bag. Begin at the top of the breast, pulling just two or three feathers at a time sharply in the direction of the head. Pull the long wing and tail feathers out singly. After plucking, singe off any remaining feathers with a lighter or candle, wipe with a damp cloth and tweak out any quills still in the skin with tweezers.

To draw   Usually a rather smelly business and one to be done as quickly as possible! Lay the bird breast side up and cut off the head. Remove the gullet and windpipe from the neck and discard, then cut off the neck and keep it for stock. Remove and discard the crop, which leads from the gullet to the base of the throat, along with any excess fat. Make a slit above the vent at the other end and with your hand gently dislodge the entrails inside the body, before pulling them out. If you wish you may keep the heart, liver and gizzard for stock. The rest should be wrapped in newspaper and thrown away. Wipe out the cavity with a damp cloth. Although pheasants are sold with the feet still on, these should be cut off just below the joint when you are preparing them for cooking.

Pheasant Broth

This is a good light soup to make from the remains of a pheasant feast. You need at least two carcasses to get the correct strength of flavour. By all means add other vegetables apart from those listed below – a little shredded leek would go well, or some potato. The main thing is to cut all the vegetables into julienne strips or fine slices and remember that this is a light broth, not a main course peasant-style soup.

Serves 4

2 or more cooked pheasant
  carcasses
1 medium onion
bayleaf
few black peppercorns

parsley stalks
2½ pints (1.4 litres) cold water
1 large carrot
1 medium courgette
2 sticks celery

Pick the meat off the carcasses and keep it in the fridge. Wash any dirt off the onion and quarter it, keeping the skin on. Put the carcasses in a saucepan with the bayleaf, peppercorns, onion and parsley and pour on the water. Bring to the boil, skimming off any scum that rises to the surface, then cover and leave to simmer gently for 2 hours or more (or use a pressure cooker). You should end up with about 1¼-2 pints (850 ml–1.1 litres).

Strain the stock. (It is always worth reaching this stage even if you are not planning to eat the soup immediately. Simply freeze it – pheasant bones are far too rare and tasty a treat to be thrown out before using for stock.) Peel the carrot and slice it thinly lengthways, then cut these wedges into matchstick strips. Do the same with the courgette and celery. Add the carrot to the soup and simmer for a few minutes before adding the other vegetables. Simmer for a further 5 minutes, test for seasoning and serve.

Pheasant Pâté

Since this pâté freezes well it is an excellent dish to make in advance, ready for the busy Christmas period. Boil the carcass up for a couple of hours to make a strong stock to store in the freezer, too.

Serves 8

1 pheasant, plucked and drawn
12 oz (335 g) pork belly
2 oz (55 g) chicken livers
½ medium onion

3 tbsp brandy
about 8oz (225 g) streaky bacon
1 large egg
black pepper

Remove all the skin from the pheasant carcass and then cut the meat from the bone using a small sharp knife. Pull out any tough tendons from the leg meat, and chop very finely by hand or in a food processor. Empty the minced meat into a mixing bowl.

Cut the rinds off the pork belly and slice into large chunks. Chop finely with the chicken livers and onion. Add to the mixing bowl, sprinkle with the brandy, mix well and leave for 1½-2 hours to marinate.

Using the blunt edge of a knife, stretch the bacon rashers so they are really thin and use them to line a 1½ pint (850 ml) terrine dish or loaf tin. Mix a beaten egg into the pheasant mixture with plenty of black pepper before filling the terrine dish. Fold the ends of bacon over the top and cover with a double thickness of silver foil. Cook in a bain marie (roasting tin half-filled with hot water) for 1¼ hours at Gas 3/325°F/170°C.

Transfer the pâté dish from the bain marie to a large plate, put heavy weights or tins on top of the foil and leave in the fridge overnight until chilled and well pressed down. Slice and serve with toast.

Pheasant and Fennel Casserole

In this unusual combination, the slightly aniseed flavour of the fennel is a good contrast to the gamey taste of a well hung pheasant.

Serves 3-4

1 pheasant, plucked, drawn and
   jointed
8 oz (225 g) fennel bulb
½ medium onion
2 sticks celery
2 oz (55 g) butter
1 tbsp wholemeal flour
¼ pint (150 ml) dry white wine
bayleaf

black pepper

Stock
rest of the pheasant carcass
½ onion
2 carrots
bayleaf
seasoning
water to cover

Put the pheasant carcass into a pan with all the other ingredients for the stock and bring to the boil. Skim, then leave at a gentle simmer while you prepare the casserole.

Trim and slice the fennel, cutting out the tough inner core. Slice the onion and celery sticks. Sauté the pheasant pieces in the butter in a flameproof casserole over a high heat until nicely browned. Lift out and set aside. Lower the heat and gently fry the vegetables, covered, for 5 minutes before stirring in the flour to absorb the fat. Gradually add the wine, stirring well to avoid lumps and add about a soup ladle of the pheasant stock. Return the pieces of pheasant to the casserole, add the bayleaf and season well with black pepper. Leave in an oven preheated to

Gas 3/325°F/170°C for 45 minutes until tender.

Continue cooking the rest of the pheasant stock and freeze it for later use.

Boned Stuffed Pheasant

Many people despair at the thought of boning a bird, thinking it is far too complex for their skills. Once you have thought through the basic anatomy of a game bird, however, it is remarkably easy if you have a small sharp knife. With its delicious chestnut stuffing, this dish will stretch a hen pheasant to serve at least four.

Serves 4

1 hen pheasant, plucked and drawn	2 tbsp fresh chopped parsley
6 oz (170 g) peeled chestnuts	2 tbsp dry white wine
1 pint (550 ml) stock	seasoning
¼ medium onion	2 oz (55 g) butter
½ oz (15 g) butter	1-2 tbsp sunflower oil

Put the chestnuts on to cook in the stock, and simmer until tender (about 30 minutes). Take the pheasant and cut off the wing ends if this has not already been done. Pull off any surplus feathers still clinging to the skin and wipe well.

Make a shallow cut through the skin along the centre back of the bird (flat side). Using short sharp strokes with your knife, work the flesh away from the bone on one side until you reach the leg. Cut the flesh away from the leg bones (you may need scissors to cut some of the tougher tendons), remove the leg bone entirely. Repeat on the other side. The important thing is not to cut through the skin or the stuffing will leak out, apart from that it doesn't matter if it looks a bit ragged. Push the legs inside out so they are lying on the inside of the bird.

Drain the chestnuts and chop very finely in a food processor or by hand. Chop the onion and sauté for a few minutes in the butter, then mix with the chestnut, parsley, wine and seasoning. Spread this over the inside of the bird, roll up tightly and tie with string, preferably wrapping the whole thing in muslin first. This prevents the bird from unrolling during cooking.

Roast in a little butter and oil at Gas 6/400°F/200°C for 35 minutes until the juices run clear. Carve with a very sharp knife. This is equally good hot or cold.

Pheasant and Apricot Casserole

In the Middle East it is quite common to cook dried fruits like apricots or raisins with meat, usually lamb. Here I have tried them with pheasant, which has a strong enough taste not to be overwhelmed by the sweetness of the fruit. The apricots need to be put in to soak in advance.

Serves 3-4

1 pheasant, plucked and drawn
4 oz (110 g) dried apricots
1 glass white wine
1 onion
2 oz (55 g) butter
1 tbsp wholemeal flour
½ tsp ground cinnamon
2 oz (55 g) raisins

seasoning

Stock
pheasant carcass
¼ onion
1 carrot
bayleaf
black peppercorns
water to cover

Joint the pheasant to give 2 whole leg joints and 2 breasts with top of the wing, the latter off the bone. Put the rest of the carcass in a saucepan with the other stock ingredients and simmer for an hour, covered, until a good flavour is obtained. If you leave the onion skin on, the colour will be much stronger. Soak the apricots in the wine for several hours.

Finely chop the onion and soften it in the butter. Turn up the heat and brown the pheasant joints. Stir in the flour, cinnamon, raisins, and the apricots with their soaking liquid and pour on the stock to just cover the pheasant. Season lightly and bring to a simmer, then cover and transfer to an oven preheated to Gas 3/325°F/170°C for 45 minutes until the meat is tender. Serve with brown rice.

Pheasant Breasts Deluxe

This makes a rather extravagant dish using a whole pheasant to serve two people. Apart from the making of the stock for the sauce, which can be left to simmer by itself, it is pretty quick to prepare and can be done at the last minute.

Serves 2

1 pheasant, plucked and drawn
3 glasses red wine
2 pints (1.1 litres) water
1 onion
2 carrots
bayleaf

black peppercorns
1 oz (30 g) butter
2 tbsp brandy
1 tsp cornflour (optional)
seasoning
squeeze lemon juice

Burn any stray feathers off the bird and cut off the two breasts with the plump top part of the wings. Return the breasts to the fridge. Put the rest of the bird into a saucepan, with the wine, water, quartered onion and carrots, bayleaf and black peppercorns. Bring to the boil, skim, and leave to simmer for 3 hours or more. Check occasionally to make sure the water level isn't getting too low, but since the eventual aim is to be left with a teacupful of stock, don't add extra water unless it's getting dry.

After this time strain the stock and reduce it to the required volume by fast boiling, if necessary. Sauté the pheasant breasts in the butter, which should be really hot, for about 3 minutes on each side. They should still be a little pink (though not uncooked) inside. Remove them and keep warm. Pour the brandy into the sauté pan – it will flame up so stand well back – then add the stock. If you like your sauce thickened, stir in the cornflour dissolved in a tablespoon of water at this point. Return to the boil, stirring, taste for seasoning, add the lemon juice and pour over the pheasant breasts.

Serve with puréed celeriac or parsnips with orange (see recipe on page 163). If you want to be less wasteful, you could pick the meat off the carcass and add it to a risotto or similar dish.

Sweetcorn

Maize, of which sweetcorn is the variety most suitable for serving as a vegetable, came to Europe in the sixteenth century from Latin America, where it has been grown for thousands of years. One of the most deeply etched memories of my travels in Peru is of the Indian women dressed in large, brightly coloured skirts over several equally brilliant petticoats, who run up to trains at every stop to sell bags of popcorn through the windows to the passengers. Popcorn was just as popular when the Incas ruled as it is now – it was not invented with the modern American teenager. In South America there are dozens of sorts of maize, the most attractive being the deep purple variety used to make a delicious soft drink called *chicha morada*.

In Europe the new corn thrived, particularly in Italy and Spain, for it likes hot sunny weather. Here in Britain it did not fare so well until modern strains were developed more suited to our northern climate. Once picked, its high sugar content quickly converts to starch, which is why home-grown sweetcorn is so much tastier than shop-bought, and why the imported kinds available out of season are really not worth buying. For the same reason sweetcorn should not be stored long at home before eating, which can tend to happen if you are tempted by the incredibly low prices to be found in high season. This can easily be avoided if you have at your disposal a range of interesting ways to serve it, other than simply on the cob.

If you are buying sweetcorn from a shop, go for individual cobs, complete with husks, that have plump juicy-looking kernels. These are more likely to be locally grown and fresher (as well as much cheaper) than the neat packaged pairs bought in supermarkets.

To prepare for cooking whole, strip off the outer husks. These are used in central America for making *tamales*, when food is wrapped in the softened husks before steaming or baking in the fire, but otherwise they should be discarded. Remove the silky threads and trim the stem end if necessary. If freshly picked, boil the cobs for just 5-10 minutes, shop-bought ones need longer. Don't salt the water in either case. To eat, pierce a skewer or fork through the stem end (you can also buy special corn-holders), before rolling in butter and black pepper and gnawing off the kernels.

In season, when sweetcorn is at its cheapest, it is worth freezing it, either whole or stripped off the cob, to be used at great savings in other recipes throughout the year. First remove all the outer husk. Then hold the cob upright and with a small sharp knife cut off all the lower kernels in short downward strokes – don't try and saw them all off in one go or cut too deeply, as this makes much harder work. They tend to fly around a bit, so do this on a large surface.

Turn the cob the other way up and repeat. The kernels usually come off slightly broken, so you may prefer to use them in soups and flans rather than serving as an unadorned vegetable – although the taste is unimpaired and far better than the tinned variety. One cob gives 3-5 oz (85-140 g) of kernels.

Incidentally, don't make the mistake I once did, while living as an impoverished student in Switzerland, of thinking you can gather a free meal from the fields of maize grown by some farms. This is used for cattle fodder and is a different variety altogether – very tough indeed!

Sweetcorn Soup

You can use frozen kernels or ones fresh from the cob for this thick warming soup. A homemade chicken stock is preferable to a cube.

Serves 4-5

3 sweetcorn cobs or 12 oz (335 g) kernels	1 oz (30 g) butter
	bayleaf
1 medium onion	2 pints (1.1 litres) chicken stock
2 medium potatoes (6 oz/170 g)	seasoning
1 clove garlic	1 tbsp fresh chopped parsley

Chop the onion, peel and chop the potato and remove the kernels from the cobs if necessary. Heat the butter in a saucepan and sauté the onion, crushed garlic and diced potato for 5 minutes. Add the sweetcorn, bayleaf and stock, bring to the boil and simmer for 25-30 minutes. A slight scum may rise to the surface, which you should skim off with a slotted spoon. Remove the bayleaf, test for seasoning and serve sprinkled with the parsley.

Sweetcorn and Rice Salad

All too often a variation on this salad is served up at buffets, where the basic ingredients have been put together so carelessly that the dish remains virtually uneaten. The sweetcorn is tinned, the rice white, overcooked and mushy, the whole thing drowned in a dressing that was poured on hours before. Try this recipe and notice the difference in texture. Everything should have a slight bite to it and the dressing be just enough to add a faint sheen and hint of extra flavour.

Serves 4

6-8 oz (170-225 g) sweetcorn kernels

6 oz (170 g) brown rice

½ medium red pepper

1 oz (30 g) hazelnuts, almonds or unsalted cashew nuts

2 tbsp fresh chopped parsley

French dressing (see page 181)

Boil the sweetcorn kernels for 5-10 minutes till cooked but still *al dente*. (If you are using ones from your freezer this may not be necessary.) Drain and put into a salad bowl. Put the rice on to cook in slightly salted boiling water, the easy cook variety will take 25-30 minutes, the ordinary kind about 40-45 minutes.

Deseed and chop the red pepper, chop the nuts coarsely and add both to the sweetcorn with the parsley. Drain the rice, rinse it under cold running water and shake the sieve to get rid of any excess water before adding to the salad. Not more than 20 minutes or so before serving stir in the French dressing.

Sweetcorn Fritters

The recipe for this is a basic pancake batter into which the sweetcorn kernels have been beaten. Traditionally served with Chicken Maryland, it is originally an American recipe, but goes equally well with other poultry dishes like Poussins with Sautéed Peppers (see page 139).

Serves 4

12 oz (335 g) sweetcorn kernels	1 egg
4 oz (110 g) unbleached plain flour	¼ pint (150 ml) milk
pinch salt	sunflower oil or oil and butter for
small pinch grated nutmeg	frying

Bring a pan of water to the boil, drop in the sweetcorn and simmer for 5-10 minutes until tender. Drain and set aside.

Sift the flour into a large bowl and add the salt and nutmeg. Make a well in the centre, whisk the egg lightly and pour it into the well, followed gradually by half the milk, drawing in the flour slowly and then beating well until really smooth. (You can use an electric whisk here.) Add the sweetcorn and the rest of the milk and beat again until smooth. Leave to stand for 30 minutes.

Heat about 1 inch (2.5 cm) oil, or oil and butter in a frying pan that is not too shallow. Stir the sweetcorn batter and drop spoonfuls of it into the pan, flatten slightly and fry until golden brown. You can turn them over carefully with a fish slice to brown the other side. Serve quickly, or keep warm until they are all cooked. Don't cover them or they will lose their crispness.

Sweetcorn Flan

The kernels should still have a slight bite when you eat this, to give a good contrast of textures. After you've tried this recipe, you'll never want to use tinned sweetcorn again, as you can really taste the freshness.

Serves 6-8

12 oz (335 g) sweetcorn kernels	black pepper
1 small red pepper	
3 rashers bacon	**Shortcrust pastry**
4 eggs	4½ oz (125 g) wholemeal flour
4 oz (110 g) fromage frais	1½ oz (40 g) unbleached plain
1 tbsp fresh thyme leaves or good	flour
pinch dried	3 oz (85 g) butter
small pinch salt	3 tbsp cold water

First make the pastry in the usual way, either in a food processor or by hand. Chill it for 30 minutes.

Boil the sweetcorn kernels for 5-10 minutes until cooked, but still slightly *al dente*. Drain and set aside. Deseed and slice the red pepper and de-rind and dice the bacon. In a bowl beat together the eggs, fromage frais, herbs and seasoning until completely smooth.

Roll out the pastry quite thinly and line a greased quiche tin of 10 inches (25 cm) diameter. Chill it a further 10 minutes, while you preheat the oven to Gas 5/375°F/190°C. Scatter the sweetcorn, bacon and red pepper all over the pastry base. Pour the egg mixture in and spread it with a spoon into every crevice.

Bake 45 minutes until golden brown and set, serve hot or cold.

Sweetcorn Relish

I always find the relishes set out on the table in American hamburger restaurants much more attractive than the hamburgers themselves. The sweetcorn one is my favourite – here is a recipe for a homemade variety, which is much less sweet and glutinous than the sort you see on sale in jars. It is also a very cheap way of making a popular relish.

Makes about 4 lb (1.8 kg)

6 sweetcorn cobs or about 1½ lb
　(670 g) kernels
1 red pepper
1 green pepper
2 whole chillies
¼ white cabbage
2 medium onions

1 tsp celery seeds
2 level tsp dry mustard
2 tsp salt
2-4 tbsp clear honey to taste
1¼-1½ pints (700-850 ml)
　distilled malt vinegar

Strip the kernels from the cobs in the usual way. Deseed the red and green peppers and the chillies (watch you don't transfer any chilli juice to your mouth or eyes) and chop finely. Remove the core from the cabbage and chop the rest finely. Peel and chop the onions. Put the vegetables into a suitable saucepan with all the other ingredients and stir well over a gentle heat until the honey is dissolved. Then leave to simmer for about 20 minutes until the vegetables are soft and the mixture thick. Pour into hot 1 lb (450 g) airtight jars and seal, before labelling and storing in the usual way (see Pickles and Chutneys).

Once opened each jar should be kept in the fridge and used quite quickly.

Sweet Peppers

Sweet peppers are yet another vegetable we must thank the New World for. Along with its cousin the chilli pepper, the sweet pepper can be found in a bewildering variety of shapes, sizes, colours and degrees of hotness in Latin American marketplaces, making the street blaze with colour. Here in Britain it is of a more uniform size and shape, either squarish, which is ideal for stuffing, or slightly more elongated.

The best season for peppers is early autumn, when the prices drop considerably. Incidentally, there is usually quite a sharp difference in price between peppers sold in supermarkets and those in greengrocers or markets, which are cheaper. This is partly because the supermarkets tend to concentrate on the high quality Class 1 specimens, whereas vegetable stallholders have found that the public is quite willing to pay less for ones that are slightly damaged, irregularly shaped, or just beginning to lose their shiny firmness. These are the sort to snap up in quantity and use in the kitchen in all kinds of different ways.

Green peppers can be rather bland, or sometimes even bitter. Left to ripen on the plant, they gradually turn yellow, then orange and finally red. Once picked they tend to wrinkle before they can complete this process. Personally I prefer red ones, which are sweeter and absolutely delicious when cooked. There are also varieties which stay yellow when fully ripe, and even one which turns almost black.

Although sweet peppers arrived in Europe some centuries ago, it was the East Europeans who adopted them first, using them in their famous goulashes and pickles, and making paprika by drying and grinding them to a powder. Here in Britain they have only really become popular in the past two decades. Spain and Italy grew enthusiastic more quickly, and in northern Spain it is a common sight to see long rows of red peppers strung along the fronts of houses to dry ready for the winter.

Peppers are easy to prepare. You only need remove the stem, plus the seeds and white pithy ribs inside. They are also rich in vitamin C and freeze well, with little deterioration in flavour.

To skin a pepper, as required for some recipes, grill under a high heat, turning occasionally, until the skin is black and blistered. Rub the now-flaky skin off under cold running water. Alternatively, the pepper can be blackened by holding it impaled on a fork in the gas flame of your stove, but the disadvantage of this is that you cannot busy yourself doing something else in the meantime.

Sweet peppers combine well with sweetcorn, as in the recipes for Sweetcorn Flan and Sweetcorn Relish. See also Asparagus Salad.

Red Pepper Soup

You can make this soup spicy hot with the addition of cayenne pepper, but it is just as good with a teaspoon of paprika to intensify the sweet pepper taste. A liquidizer or food processor is needed. Choose fresh peppers with really smooth skins to obtain the best flavour.

Serves 4

3 large red peppers
½ medium onion
2 tbsp sunflower oil
½ level tsp cayenne or paprika
3 medium tomatoes

1¼ pints (700 ml) chicken stock
bayleaf
squeeze lemon juice
1 tbsp freshly chopped coriander or
    parsley

Wipe the peppers and put them, whole, under a hot grill until they are blistered. Cool them and rub or scrape off the now loose skins, using a small sharp knife. It is best to do this over the sink, as it helps to hold the pepper under the cold tap occasionally. Halve, remove the seeds and chop finely.

Chop the onion finely and sauté it with the peppers and cayenne or paprika in the oil for 5 minutes. Peel the tomatoes, blanching them first in boiling water to loosen the skins, then quarter them and remove the pips. Chop finely and add with the stock and a bayleaf to the peppers. Bring to the boil and simmer, covered, for 10-15 minutes.

Liquidize the soup and add a squeeze of fresh lemon juice before serving sprinkled with the chopped coriander or parsley.

Scallop and Sweet Pepper Salad

It is fun to prepare a dish which uses peppers of all the different colours. Here they make a very pretty first course salad, mixed with lightly poached scallops and lime or lemon juice. Use fresh scallops or good quality frozen ones.

Serves 4

1 red, 1 green and 1 yellow pepper
4-6 fresh scallops (depending on
    size) or 1 lb (450 g) frozen
little shellfish stock or
    court bouillon

French dressing using fresh lime or
    lemon juice instead of
    vinegar (see page 181)
seasoning

Remove the scallops from their shells and rinse out any sand. Put them into a small saucepan with a little shellfish stock or court bouillon from the freezer (water and white wine will do) and poach very gently for just 3 minutes until they have turned white. Remove and leave to cool.

Deseed the peppers and slice quite thinly. Blanch them for 2 minutes in boiling water to soften slightly (time them from the moment the water returns to the boil). Slice the scallops horizontally into three or four and mix with the peppers. Toss in a vinaigrette made of olive oil and fresh lime or lemon juice, season and serve.

Poussins with Sautéed Peppers

You need a good sauté pan or thick-bottomed flameproof casserole for this dish, because the initial cooking must be done over a really high heat to extract the best taste from the peppers. You could use just red peppers, but the multi-coloured effect is visually very appealing.

Serves 4

2 red, 2 green and 2 yellow peppers
2 poussins, about 14-16 oz
  (390-450 g) each
2 tbsp sunflower oil
1 oz (30 g) butter
1 medium onion

2-3 cloves garlic
¼ pint (150 ml) dry white wine
seasoning
pinch dried thyme
2 tbsp fresh chopped coriander

Using a pair of poultry shears or strong kitchen scissors, cut the poussins in half lengthways, right down the breast and backbone. Heat the oil and butter in a heavy pan and sauté the birds over a very high heat until well browned. The idea is to sear them, not cook them yet. Remove and put on one side.

Halve the peppers, remove the seeds and cores and slice them, not too finely. Slice the onion and sauté it in the pan over a high heat with the crushed garlic and peppers for 5 minutes. Lower the heat, replace the poussins and add the white wine, some seasoning and a generous pinch of thyme. Simmer, covered, for about 15 minutes until the juices run clear when pricked with a fork. Serve sprinkled with the coriander for a distinctive taste.

Spanish Stuffed Peppers

This is a delicious dish which I found served all over the north-east corner of Spain, especially in the Rioja area. Discouraged by the rather watery version you tend to get in Britain, I initially skipped past the Pimientos Rellenos on the restaurant menus. Once I had been persuaded to try them, however, I was amazed by the difference. The secret is to skin the peppers, which gives a smooth, mouth-watering result and also eliminates the rather bitter taste that peppers sometimes have. Some people use green peppers, but red ones tend to be sweeter and tastier.

Serves 4

4 medium regular-shaped
  red peppers
8 oz (225 g) minced pork
8 oz (225 g) minced lamb
1 medium onion
1 tbsp sunflower oil
1 egg
seasoning

Tomato sauce

½ medium onion
1 large clove garlic
1 tbsp olive oil
1 lb (450 g) ripe tomatoes or a
  14 oz (390 g) tin
2 tbsp fresh chopped parsley
seasoning
1 tbsp wine vinegar

Skin the peppers after grilling them in the normal way, keeping them whole. Carefully cut off the top of each one and scoop out the seeds, being sure not to split the flesh. Wedge them, open side up, in an ovenproof dish.

Chop the onion. Heat the oil in a sauté or frying pan and fry the onion for a couple of minutes. Add the minced meat and stir over a fairly high heat for 4-5 minutes. Remove from the heat and cool slightly, then pour off any liquid. Mix in a beaten egg and season. Stuff the mixture into the peppers.

To make the tomato sauce, chop the onion and soften it in the oil with the crushed garlic in a small saucepan. Add the other ingredients, skinning the tomatoes and chopping them if you are using fresh ones. (Dip into boiling water for 10 seconds then into cold to loosen the skins.) Cover and simmer for 20 minutes over a low heat. Cool slightly and liquidize, then pour over the stuffed peppers.

Bake the dish, covered, in an oven preheated to Gas 4/350°F/180°C for 40 minutes.

If you are unable to find minced pork and lamb in your supermarket, buy shoulder fillet or a similar cut and finely chop it using a very sharp knife or a food processor (being careful not to process it to a paste).

Braised Paprika Beef with Peppers

A good warming dish for those autumn evenings when the nights are drawing in, this is simple to prepare and can be left to cook.

Serves 4

2 large red peppers	2 level tbsp paprika
4 pieces braising steak, total about 1½ lb (670 g)	½ pint (300 ml) beef stock
1 medium onion	2 level tbsp cornflour
2 tbsp olive or sunflower oil	4 tbsp cold water

Slice the onion and sauté in the oil in a frying pan until browned. Remove to an ovenproof dish and stir in the paprika. Quickly sauté the pieces of braising steak in the hot oil until just browned on both sides to seal. Transfer these to the dish containing the onions, pour the hot stock into the frying pan, swirl round and pour over the meat. Cover and braise for 1¼-1½ hours in the centre of an oven preheated to Gas 4/350°F/180°C.

Halve and deseed the peppers and slice them thinly. Add to the casserole after the cooking time given above and leave a further 30 minutes. Just before the end of cooking stir in the cornflour, mixed to a

paste with the cold water and put the dish back in the oven. As it returns
to a simmer the gravy will thicken.

Serve with plain boiled or baked potatoes to mop up the delicious,
slightly spicy, juice.

Pickled Red Peppers

This is a lovely bright-coloured pickle, quick and easy to make. It does
not keep very long though, so make it in small batches, as below,
throughout the late summer and autumn when peppers are at their
cheapest. The pepper slices turn out quite soft, but if you prefer them
crisper, don't blanch the peppers, just boil the vinegar for 10-15 minutes,
strain and pour over.

Makes 1 medium Kilner jar

3 large firm red peppers
2 bayleaves
6 cardammon pods
thick slice fresh ginger
½ tsp whole coriander seeds

1 inch (2.5 cm) stick cinnamon
1 tsp black peppercorns
just over 1 pint (550 ml)
  white wine vinegar

Quarter the peppers lengthways and cut out the stem and any pithy white
flesh, shaking out the seeds. Slice thickly. Break up the bayleaves, de-
husk the cardammon pods and bruise the ginger. Bring the vinegar and
all the spices to the boil and simmer gently for 10 minutes, closely
covered. Add the red pepper slices, stir well, return to the boil and
blanch for 2 minutes.

Remove the peppers to a clean jar. Strain the vinegar and pour it over
the slices, before sealing. Store for about 2 weeks before eating and use
up within 6 weeks of making.

Avocados

The avocado originated in Latin America, where the Aztecs called it
ahuacatl. The Spanish conquistadors brought it back to Europe and it first
became known in Britain in the seventeenth century. Until the 1960s,
however, few people in this country had seen let alone tasted one. It took
the marketing skills of the Israelis to introduce the avocado to our tables
and restaurants, where unfortunately it is all too often served underripe
and with little imagination.

In Guatemala I have seen huge avocado trees beside the road with
large nets strung from their lower branches to catch the windfalls.
Commercially grown avocados, however, are picked before they are ripe
and often sold in a similar condition. Except for extreme cases, an
avocado should ripen in two to three days stored out of the light in a
warm place (kitchen or airing cupboard). When ready to eat it will yield
slightly when gently squeezed in your hand and be especially soft near the
top. It can now be transferred to the bottom of the fridge to prevent it
from over-ripening.

Avocados are not part of the pear family, and only have this tacked
on to their name because of their shape. Even then it is rather
misleading, as some can be almost round. The small green-black knobbly
skinned varieties are just as good as the larger smooth-skinned green
ones. Although avocados thrive in all tropical and sub-tropical
countries, those sold in Britain come principally from Israel and South
Africa.

At certain times of the year, particularly in late winter, they are at the
height of their season and can be picked up especially cheaply from
market stalls. It is also possible to buy them at knock-down prices if they
are slightly damaged or almost too ripe, since they spoil so quickly.
Although an avocado can be delicious, if in perfect condition, served
simply with a first-class French dressing, this is the time to experiment
with other ways of preparing it. Avocado can be baked (20-30 minutes

depending on size at Gas 6/400°F/200°C), cooked in soups, made into dips and sandwich fillings, or used in a multitude of salads. Avocados contain more protein than any other fruit (as well as more fat) and are rich in vitamins A and B.

Guacamole

This delicious and by now well known avocado dip comes originally from Mexico – *aguaca* being the Nahuatl Indian word for avocado and *mole* (pronounced moll-eh) meaning sauce. The true version is made from avocados mashed together with chillies, chopped fresh coriander and lime juice. The one more easily made in Britain uses lemon juice, Tabasco and is sometimes even stretched to feed more by the addition of cream cheese. Here I give both versions – if you can get the ingredients compare the first with the second and taste the difference.

Whichever version you use, make sure your avocados are really ripe. It is easier to make this in a food processor or with an electric whisk, but purists say it is best made by hand in a mortar and pestle. This is an excellent way of using up avocados that are just past peak condition.

Mexican Guacamole

2 large ripe avocados   seasoning
½ small onion   2-3 tbsp fresh chopped coriander
1 fresh chilli   juice of 2 limes
1 small clove garlic

Halve and stone the avocados. Peel by running the metal handle of a teaspoon round between the skin and the flesh – you will now be able to turn out the flesh quite easily. Peel the onion and chop it finely with the deseeded chilli and garlic clove, adding the avocado in chunks and processing or beating until smooth. Stir in the seasoning (lots of black pepper and a fair pinch of salt make a real difference if your avocados are a bit bland), the coriander and the lime juice.

The lime should prevent the mixture from discolouring, but should it do so don't worry. Just beat well immediately before serving and the discoloured parts will be mixed into the fresh pale green flesh underneath.

British Avocado Dip

1 large avocado   juice of ½ lemon
½ small onion   few drops Tabasco sauce
1 small clove garlic   a little olive oil
2 oz (55 g) low-fat cream cheese or   seasoning
   fromage frais

Peel the avocado and remove the stone in the usual way. Finely chop the onion with the garlic clove and beat in the avocado flesh, cream cheese, lemon juice and Tabasco, seasoning well. If the mixture is a little stiff, mix in a teaspoon or two of olive oil. Again, the citrus juice should prevent the dip from turning colour before serving.

Avocado and Pernod Soup

There are many variations on avocado soup, all based on stock and cream. I find that on top of the fairly rich taste of avocado, half a pint of cream is too much (some recipes even suggest using double cream !) Instead I use half yoghurt, half single cream, and to sharpen up the taste a bit more, add a little Pernod, the French aniseed yellow spirit. If you don't have any of this, or don't like the taste, substitute dry sherry.

Serves 4

2 medium avocados	dash Tabasco
small tub (150 g) natural yoghurt	seasoning
¼ pint (150 ml) single cream	1 tbsp Pernod or dry sherry
1 pint (550 ml) good chicken stock	1 tbsp fresh chopped coriander
1-2 tsp fresh lemon juice	

I wouldn't advise trying to make this without a liquidizer or food processor, it would take forever and even then might be rather lumpy.

Halve the avocados and remove the stones. Scoop the flesh into the machine, making sure you include all the bright green bit next to the skin which provides the essential colour. Process the avocado flesh with the yoghurt until smooth, then add all the other ingredients. If you have just made the chicken stock, cool it slightly before adding.

Taste for seasoning and either serve hot or chilled, sprinkled with chopped coriander. Don't make it too far in advance or it will start to turn brown. If there is any slight discolouration when you take it out of the fridge, simply stir the soup well.

Avocado with Strawberry Sauce

This is an excellent and unusual starter. It has to be made at the last minute, but takes only a very short time to prepare. You need a liquidizer or food processor to make the sauce. Raspberries can be used instead of strawberries.

Serves 4

2 ripe avocados	3-4 tbsp French dressing made with
8 oz (225 g) fresh or frozen	lemon juice instead of vinegar
strawberries or raspberries	(see page 181)
	small bunch of watercress

Whizz the hulled strawberries up in a liquidizer with the French dressing. This can be done in advance, but you will need to give it a final whizz before using in case it has separated.

Halve the avocados and remove the stone. Run the metal handle of a teaspoon round between the skin and the flesh and then turn the avocado upside-down, pushing with your thumbs to get the flesh out in one piece. Flood 4 side-plates with the sauce, then cut each avocado half lengthways into 5 or 6 slices. Arrange these in a fan shape on top of the sauce, garnish with a little washed watercress and serve immediately.

Avocado and Mango Salad

Avocado goes well in all sorts of salads, adding a good contrast to both the texture and taste of most crisp salad ingredients. But why not try this as an unusual starter – half-fruit half-avocado served in pretty glass dishes. Choose avocados that are ripe but still firm, or they will become mushy when you mix the salad together.

Serves 4
2 medium avocados
1 small grapefruit

1 mango
juice of 1 lime

Halve the grapefruit and cut out the segments with a grapefruit knife, or otherwise segment it as you would an orange, by topping and tailing and cutting away all the skin before slicing down between the membranes. Peel the mango, holding it over a bowl to catch the juice, and slice the flesh off the central core. Dice roughly. Peel the avocados by running the handle of a metal teaspoon round between the skin and the flesh – the whole half avocado should fall out quite easily. Slice and add to the bowl with the grapefruit and mango. Pour on the lime juice and mix lightly. The citrus juice will prevent the avocado flesh discolouring, so this salad can be made some time in advance.

Stuffed Avocados (Paltas Rellenos)

This dish is filling enough to be served as a main course with salads, particularly if you include some chopped chicken. It was the first dish I ever ordered when I arrived in Peru at the beginning of a six-month visit, and I found that however basic the restaurant seemed, or however remote the town, this dish always came up trumps. The ingredients can vary considerably depending on what is available, but those below form a combination that works well.

If you want to serve it as a starter, halve the quantities (within reason

– don't get into miniscule fractions), and use two and a half avocados.

Serves 4

4½ large avocados	pinch chilli powder
1 medium carrot	1 cooked chicken breast (optional)
2 tbsp shelled peas	juice of ½ lemon
2 eggs	½ tsp French mustard
3 sticks celery	3-4 tbsp mayonnaise
1 tbsp green olives	2 tbsp fresh chopped parsley
seasoning	

Peel and dice the carrot and cook it in a little water until tender. Simmer the peas until cooked and drain. Hardboil the eggs. Cut the avocados in half and remove the stones. Run a metal teaspoon handle round between the flesh and the skin and then turn them upside-down. With a little pressure from your fingers the inside should come out in one piece. Mash one half in a mixing bowl, set the others to one side.

Add the carrots and peas to the mashed avocado. Finely slice the celery, de-stone and chop the olives and mix in with the other vegetables, adding the seasoning, chilli and chopped cooked chicken if you are using it. Slice the hardboiled eggs.

Beat the lemon juice into the mayonnaise with the mustard and stir it into the vegetables. Pile all this into the avocado halves, decorate with the egg slices, sprinkle with parsley and serve on a bed of shredded lettuce.

Baked Avocado with Crab

Few people think of baking avocados, imagining them always to be a salad ingredient, best when raw. However, hot avocado is very good and if you have one which is still slightly underripe, this is a good way to serve it, as cooking softens it up.

You may use frozen crabmeat very successfully here, available in packs of half-white, half-brown meat. You should include the brown for added taste.

Serves 4

2 large avocados	1 tsp tomato purée
6 oz (170 g) white crabmeat	1 dsp wholemeal flour
2 oz (55 g) brown crabmeat	1 tsp mild curry powder
1 medium onion	4-5 tbsp milk
1 clove garlic	black pepper
1 oz (30 g) butter	1 tbsp fresh chopped parsley

Chop the onion and sauté it with the garlic in the hot butter for 5 minutes until golden brown. Stir in the tomato purée, flour, curry powder and crabmeat and cook for a minute or two, before adding the milk to form a smooth mixture. Season with black pepper.

Cut the avocados in half and remove the stones. Slice a thin sliver off the rounded side of each half so it will sit on a baking tray without rolling around. Pile the crabmeat into the avocados, place on the tray and cover loosely with tinfoil. Bake in an oven preheated to Gas 6/400°F/200°C for 20-30 minutes, until the avocados are really soft when squeezed, but not brown.

Sprinkle with chopped parsley and serve.

Brussels Sprouts

These familiar miniature cabbages are as much a part of England as roast beef and Yorkshire pudding. Yet although they were being cultivated in Belgium as far back as the thirteenth century, they did not appear on the English table until well into the Victorian era. They are one of the main core of our native winter vegetables, and can be picked in kitchen gardens right through from September to March.

Cheap and nourishing they may be, but many people find it hard to think of ways of serving them imaginatively. In fact the British slapdash approach to both buying and cooking green vegetables reaches its nadir with sprouts, which are possibly the worst abused vegetable in the country. You should never, for example, buy yellowing sprouts, they will taste disgusting. The heads should be tight and crisp and bright green. Likewise do not overcook them – heaped plates of khaki-coloured sprouts with the taste and texture boiled away to nothing turned my stomach as a child.

The American soldiers who flooded into Britain during the war admitted they could put up with most hardships – the rationing, the bombings, the blackout – but there were two things they could never get used to, our telephone system and Brussels sprouts !

Some people cut a cross in the base to help them cook more evenly, but this is time-consuming and not really necessary if you choose the smaller sprouts, which have a finer flavour than the large ones anyway. Simmer them for just 7-8 minutes in a very little water, drain and serve with lots of black pepper. Or try the recipes below – you might even persuade a visiting ex-GI to change his opinion.

Brussels Sprouts Soup

If you make a soup based purely on Brussels sprouts the strong taste of this distinctive vegetable is rather too overwhelming. However, a good soup can be made by cooking them up with other well flavoured vegetables such as celeriac and leeks.

Serves 4

12 oz (335 g) Brussels sprouts
½ medium onion
¾ oz (20 g) butter
4 oz (110 g) celeriac (½ medium)
1 slim leek

1¼ pints (700 ml) chicken stock
bayleaf
seasoning
2 tbsp fresh chopped parsley

Trim the sprouts and quarter them, or halve if small. Slice the onion and sweat it in the butter over a gentle heat until soft. Peel and dice the celeriac, slice the leek and wash it well in a colander under running water. Add all the vegetables to the onion and cook a few more minutes, stirring occasionally, before pouring in the stock. Bring to the boil, add the bayleaf, cover and simmer for 10 minutes or until the vegetables are tender.

Remove the bayleaf and liquidize the soup briefly, but be careful not to make it over-smooth. Return to the pan, reheat and test for seasoning. Sprinkle with the chopped parsley before serving.

Brussels Sprouts with Chestnut Sauce

These two vegetables are traditionally served whole, mixed together, as a popular accompaniment to the Christmas turkey. By puréeing the chestnuts you not only end up with a tasty alternative, but also a dish that could be served as a light supper dish. The sauce can look a little dull-coloured, so enhance its appearance by sprinkling the whole dish with diced crisp bacon just before serving.

Serves 4

1½ lb (670 g) Brussels sprouts
4 oz (110 g) peeled chestnuts
½ pint (300 ml) milk
bayleaf
½ small onion

½ oz (15 g) wholemeal flour
½ oz (15 g) butter
seasoning
2 oz (55 g) back bacon

Put the chestnuts into simmering water to cook. Meanwhile trim the sprouts and make the base for the sauce, by bringing the milk to the boil with the onion and bayleaf, then leaving off the heat for 5 minutes to infuse. Strain and set aside. Make a roux with the butter and flour, and stir in the strained flavoured milk until you have a smooth sauce. Do not make it too thick at this stage.

When the chestnuts are cooked (which takes 30 minutes or so), drain and pick off any brown inner skin remaining on them. Purée in a food processor or liquidizer with the white sauce. Put the sprouts on to cook in boiling water and the de-rinded bacon under a hot grill.

Season the sauce. If it is too thick, add a little more milk. Drain the sprouts when tender, pour the hot sauce over them and sprinkle with the bacon, which should be dark and crisp, but not burnt.

Braised Brussels Sprouts with Onions

By braising sprouts in a rich stock with tiny pickling onions, their full flavour is brought out. Choose firm young sprouts and the smallest onions you can find.

Serves 4

1 lb (450 g) Brussels sprouts	2 tsp coriander seeds
4 oz (110 g) pickling onions (12)	1 small clove garlic
1 tbsp sunflower oil	½ pint (300 ml) good stock
1 oz (30 g) butter	squeeze lemon juice

Trim the sprouts and peel the onions, leaving them whole. Sauté the onions in the hot oil and butter with the coriander seeds over a high heat until golden brown, adding the crushed garlic a minute or so before the end of cooking. Add the sprouts and stock – there should be just enough to come half-way up the vegetables. Cover and braise gently on top of the stove for 10 minutes.

Lift the vegetables out of the stock into a serving dish and squeeze over a little lemon juice.

Purée of Brussels Sprouts

If you are getting bored with the sight of Brussels sprouts, here is a good way to serve them, disguised in a purée. The nutmeg adds a special flavour, but don't overdo it or it will dominate the dish.

Serves 4

1 lb (450 g) brussels sprouts	1 oz (30 g) butter
12 oz (335 g) potatoes	black pepper
1 pint (550 ml) light stock	small pinch grated nutmeg

Trim the sprouts. Peel and dice the potatoes. Bring the stock to the boil, add the potato pieces and simmer for 5 minutes. Add the sprouts and simmer another 5-10 minutes until both the vegetables are tender. Mash the two together (a food processor is best for making a really smooth purée), with the butter and seasonings. Serve really hot.

Greek Brussels Sprouts

You will never find this in Greece, but I have given this dish its title because of the Greek egg and lemon sauce the sprouts are served with.

This really lifts them into a different class and the strong flavours of the sprouts and lemon go very well together.

Serves 4

1 lb (450 g) Brussels sprouts	1 whole egg
½ pint (300 ml) chicken stock	4 tbsp lemon juice
3 egg yolks	seasoning

Prepare the Brussels sprouts and put them on to cook in a pan of boiling water. Meanwhile make the sauce. First heat up the stock. In another small saucepan, off the heat, whisk the egg yolks and whole egg until light and fluffy. Add the lemon juice, whisking all the time and then gradually the hot stock. Transfer to the stove over a very low heat and as you continue whisking, the sauce will gradually thicken. Keep it warm over the very lowest possible flame until the sprouts are cooked, then drain them and transfer to a hot dish. Pour the sauce over and serve.

On no account must the sauce boil or even simmer or the eggs will scramble.

Jerusalem Artichokes

For a vegetable that, once it has taken root, grows like a weed, Jerusalem artichoke is remarkably rarely eaten in Britain. Few people know much about it, puzzling over its strange name and shape before even reaching the stage of wondering how to cook it.

Firstly, the knobbly root vegetable has no connection with either Jerusalem or artichokes. When it was first brought back from the New World its slightly nutty flavour was likened to a globe artichoke (although this is largely only true when it is fresh from the ground). Above ground its tall flowers turn to follow the movement of the sun, so it was classed as a *girasol* (sunflower). The British, refusing to bow to fancy foreign names, soon corrupted this to Jerusalem.

Grown in my parents' garden the six-foot-high foliage was used as a windshield and the roots left very much to get on with it without much attention. The result tends to be a glut of rather knobbly roots, which take some time to scrub and peel. Commercially grown ones are now bred to have smoother skins and a more uniform shape and can be peeled more easily. Jerusalem artichokes are only available in season (from early November to March). They are at their most plentiful in December and January. Stored in the bottom of the fridge, they will stay fresh for about a week before starting to soften.

The knobbly sort are best scrubbed with a nail brush and parboiled for 5 minutes, after which the skins will slip off quite easily. Total boiling time should be 20-25 minutes – if undercooked the slight windiness they cause for some digestions will be intensified. (This drawback only affects some people, so try a small quantity if you are eating them for the first time. Even those who love them and suffer no after-effects advise that they shouldn't be eaten to excess.)

Artichoke and Scallop Soup

Jerusalem artichokes go well with scallops, and can be added to the classic, but expensive, Coquilles St Jacques à la Parisienne (scallops served on the shell with a piped border of mashed potato) to make the dish go further. Here they are combined with scallops in a delicious soup. Its rather dull colour is livened up by the bright orange of the scallop corals.

Serves 4

12 oz (335 g) Jerusalem artichokes	1 pint (550 ml) chicken stock
3 large scallops	seasoning
1 medium onion	¼ pint (150 ml) milk
1 oz (30 g) butter	2 tbsp fresh chopped parsley
6 oz (170 g) potato	

Chop the onion and cook it in the butter in a saucepan until soft. Peel and dice the artichokes and the potato and toss them in the butter for a minute or two, then lower the heat, cover the pan and cook gently for 15 minutes. Stir in the chicken stock, season lightly and simmer for a further 20 minutes.

Meanwhile cut the scallops and their coral into chunks. Liquidize the soup and stir in the milk. Add the scallops, poach lightly for 5 minutes or less, until the scallops are cooked, and served sprinkled with chopped parsley.

Roast Jerusalem Artichokes

If roasted well, this is a delicious way of serving this unusual vegetable – crisp golden skins, soft nutty-flavoured insides.

Serves 4
1¼ lb (550 g) Jerusalem artichokes   sunflower oil

Scrub the artichokes, but it is not necessary to peel them unless they are very large and tough-skinned. Put a roasting tin containing enough oil to just cover the bottom into the oven at Gas 6/400°F/200°C for 5-10 minutes, until the oil is really hot. Cut any large artichokes in half, add them all to the pan and roast for about 50 minutes until golden brown, turning occasionally. Drain well on kitchen paper and serve.

If roasted round a joint of meat, artichokes – like potatoes – may absorb the delicious juices but in doing so tend to go soggy. I prefer to leave the meat juices for making a good base for the gravy. (Another way of serving artichokes, which is excellent with roast meat, is in a béchamel sauce with a spoonful of capers mixed in.)

Buttered Artichokes with Carrots

If you sweat Jerusalem artichokes very slowly in butter they make a good tender vegetable accompaniment for most main courses. But the colour can be a bit bland, especially when served on the same plate as potatoes. Here is a way to jazz up the appearance and the taste, by adding carrots and freshly chopped coriander leaves.

Serves 4
1 lb (450 g) Jerusalem artichokes   2 oz (55 g) butter
1 lb (450 g) carrots   2 tbsp fresh chopped coriander
squeeze lemon juice   black pepper

Peel the carrots and slice them thickly into chunks. Peel the artichokes and cut them into similar-sized pieces. (Keep them in water with a squeeze of lemon until ready to use to prevent them from discolouring.) Heat the butter in a saucepan and add both vegetables, stirring until they are well coated with butter. Put on the lid and sweat gently for about 30 minutes, stirring occasionally to ensure even cooking.

Sprinkle with the chopped coriander and season with black pepper before serving.

Jerusalem Artichoke 'Cakes'

Like fish cakes, these are easy to make and are a good way of camouflaging the rather dull colour of plainly boiled artichokes.

Serves 4
1 lb (450 g) Jerusalem artichokes   2 tbsp fresh chopped parsley
1 oz (30 g) butter   1 egg
1 tbsp fresh wholemeal   3-4 tbsp fine oatmeal or
   breadcrumbs   wholemeal flour
seasoning   sunflower oil for frying

Peel the artichokes, cut them into chunks and cook in boiling water until tender when pierced with a fork. Drain and mash or process in a machine while hot with the butter, breadcrumbs, seasoning and parsley. Stir in the egg and leave to go cold.

Heat enough oil in a pan for shallow frying and shake out the oatmeal or flour on to a plate. Take a scoop of the artichoke mixture and pat it between your hands until you have a flat cake about 3 inches (7.5 cm) in diameter. You should be able to make 8 cakes out of the mixture. Coat them in the oatmeal or flour and fry immediately until golden brown, turning once. This takes about 2 minutes on each side.

Serve plain or with a tomato sauce (see page 96).

Provençal Jerusalem Artichoke Gratin

Here is a colourful, tasty and quite filling way of serving Jerusalem artichokes. This could either go with simply grilled fish or even become a tasty and warming light lunch with bread and a green salad.

Serves 4

1 lb (450 g) Jerusalem artichokes
½ fennel bulb
2 tbsp olive oil
1 large clove garlic

4 tomatoes
1 tbsp fresh chopped parsley
seasoning
3 oz (85 g) Cheddar cheese

Prepare the artichokes in the normal way and cut into bite-sized pieces. Simmer them in boiling water until nearly tender – they will have a little more cooking time later on. Meanwhile trim the fennel bulb and slice it finely. Heat the oil in quite a large saucepan and sauté the fennel with the crushed garlic until nearly tender. Quarter and deseed the tomatoes and chop them roughly, then add them with the drained Jerusalem artichokes to the saucepan. Cook until the tomatoes have broken down, then add the parsley and seasoning and transfer to a shallow gratin dish. Grate the cheese and sprinkle all over and pop the dish into a hot oven or under the grill until the cheese is golden brown.

Leeks

The leek is a member of the onion family that has appeared on British plates for many centuries, apart from a fall from grace lasting from the seventeenth to early twentieth century, when the stage was stolen by previously unknown vegetables arriving from the New World.

Old, oversized, insufficiently washed or overcooked leeks can put you off this delicious vegetable for life. There is an obsession in many parts of Britain, particularly in the north-east, with growing giant leeks to beat the record (currently about 9½ lbs). Whilst risking offending these industrious gardeners, I can only say that the slimmer the leek, the more tender it is and the more delicate its flavour. In this country it is still difficult to buy leeks in the summer, when they are young and sweet and ideal for things like Vichyssoise soup. Here it is very much a winter vegetable, with its high season being November to late February.

That said, well chosen leeks are an excellent addition to the rather sparse winter vegetable basket. Select ones that have a good proportion of white to green stalk, and preferably have the roots still on, as this makes it easier to judge their freshness. Cut off the tough dark leaves at the top and make a slit (or a cross if large) about 2 inches (5 cm) down towards the root. Holding the leek upside down, wash out any grit from this top part of the stalk and then stand it root-end uppermost in a jar of cold water for 30 minutes for any remaining grit or mud to soak out. (If you are slicing your leeks, you can merely rinse them well afterwards in a colander under cold running water.)

Finally, don't overcook them, or they will be very nasty indeed – khaki green and slimy. Below are some delicious ways of eating leeks that will, I hope, dispel any lingering memories of school dinners and show you how versatile a vegetable it is.

Leek and Bacon Soup

This is a lovely tasty winter soup made a little special by the addition of the bacon, which should be unsmoked or the end-result may be rather salty. It is a good way of cooking the big leeks that are all you can find in some shops.

Serves 4

1 large or 2 medium leeks (8 oz/225 g after trimming)
½ medium onion
3 oz (85 g) back bacon
1 medium carrot
¾ oz (20 g) butter

1½ pints (850 ml) chicken stock
bayleaf
black pepper
¼ pint (150 ml) milk
2 tbsp fresh chopped parsley

Cut any tough green part off the top of the leeks, but leave the more tender bright green leaves for colour. Trim the root off, slice the leeks in half lengthways and then thinly across before washing well under running water in a colander. Chop the onion, de-rind and finely dice the bacon and coarsely grate the carrot.

Sauté the bacon and onion in the butter over quite a high heat for 2 minutes, then lower the heat, add the leek and carrot, cover with a buttered paper and sweat very gently for 5 minutes. Pour in the stock, add the bayleaf and season with black pepper – you shouldn't need salt since the bacon provides sufficient for most tastes. Bring to the boil and simmer, covered, for 10 minutes.

Add the milk and allow to cool slightly before liquidizing very briefly. Don't blend it away to a purée as this obliterates the visual effect of the tiny pieces of bacon and carrot seen in the soup. You may wish to mop up any excess butter at this point by skimming the surface with kitchen paper (or chill and spoon off the solidified butter). Reheat, sprinkle with the parsley and serve with crusty wholemeal bread.

Leeks Vinaigrette

This makes a good salad provided you take care to use the young slim leeks, not much thicker than your thumb, which are available earlier in the season.

Serves 4

6 young leeks
3 tbsp lemon juice
black pepper

6 tbsp olive oil
1 tbsp finely shredded mint leaves
few slices lemon

Cut the tough green parts off the leeks and trim the root. Make a slit lengthways into the top part and wash well in the usual way to remove any grit. Simmer, white end down, in a pan of water tall enough to cover completely with a lid so the green parts cook in the steam – this helps prevent them from overcooking and disintegrating. It should take 5-10 minutes only, so watch carefully and test with a fork to see when the leeks are tender.

In a bowl beat together the lemon juice, black pepper and oil, then add the mint. Drain the leeks, cut them into 3 or 4 chunks each, put these carefully in a dish and while still warm pour the dressing over. Leave to cool for long enough for the lemon and mint flavours to be absorbed.

Serve garnished with a few thin twisted slices of lemon.

Sautéed Leeks and Fennel

These two strong-tasting vegetables go very well together and make a good dish to accompany something like a chicken pie or a casserole.

Serves 4

12 oz (335 g) leeks, weighed
   after trimming
8 oz (225 g) fennel bulb
1-2 tbsp sunflower oil

2 cloves garlic
1 tsp ground coriander
black pepper
1 dsp fresh chopped marjoram

Trim the leeks and slice them thinly. Wash well in a colander under cold running water to get rid of any grit. Remove the stalks and the tough central core of the fennel, and slice the rest thinly. Heat the oil in a heavy-bottomed saucepan or flameproof casserole and sauté the fennel with the garlic and coriander for 5 minutes. Add the leeks, season with black pepper, lower the heat and cook a further 5 minutes, stirring occasionally.

Sprinkle with the marjoram and serve.

Leek Dumplings

We may live in an age of affluence, but many still find it hard to satisfy hungry appetites on a limited budget. It is sad how many of us are unfamiliar with the traditional recipes of our grandparents, who certainly knew how to fill the gaps for a few pennies. Dumplings, for example, are rarely eaten in Britain today, for no good reason. You can now buy vegetable suet instead of the traditional beef variety and it is very quick and easy to make up into filling dumplings. These are best added to a casserole for the last 15 minutes' cooking time, or dropped into a thick broth. I tried making them with chopped leek added, and found it gave them a rather appealing, slightly pungent flavour. A good way of using up a little leftover leek.

Serves 4 (makes 8)

3 oz (85 g) trimmed leek
2 oz (55 g) wholemeal flour
2 oz (55 g) unbleached plain flour

2 oz (55 g) shredded vegetable suet
1½ level tsp baking powder
2½ fl.oz (75 ml) cold water

Finely chop and wash the leek. Sift the flour into a large bowl and stir in the suet, baking powder and leek. Using an ordinary table knife, stir in enough water to form a light elastic dough. Turn out on to a lightly floured surface and knead gently, then cover and leave for 10 minutes.

Divide the dough into 8 small balls the size of a golfball. Drop these into a casserole 15 minutes before the end of cooking time, or cook in soup or stock for the same length of time. The dumplings will increase in volume considerably, and soak up some of the delicious juices from the casserole.

Leek and Chicken Pie

A simple pie that can be prepared in advance. If you are using leftover cooked chicken, you will need about 1¼-1½ lb (550 -670 g).

Serves 6

12 oz (335 g) trimmed leeks
4 lb (1.8 kg) chicken or 4 double
    leg joints (thigh and
    drumstick)
water
bayleaf
parsley stalks
1 carrot
1 onion
black peppercorns
½ oz (15 g) butter

½ oz (15 g) butter
½ oz (15 g) wholemeal flour
seasoning

Shortcrust pastry
4½ oz (125 g) wholemeal flour
1½ oz (45 g) unbleached plain
    flour
3 oz (85 g) butter
pinch salt
2-3 tbsp cold water
beaten egg

If using a whole chicken, quarter it. Put the pieces into a saucepan with
enough water to cover, the bayleaf, parsley, quartered carrot, quartered
onion (leave the skin on) and peppercorns. Bring to the boil, skim, lower
the heat and simmer for 20-25 minutes. Remove the joints and boil the
stock down to about ½ pint (300 ml).

Make the pastry in the usual way, either in a food processor or by
hand, and leave to chill in the fridge. Wash the leeks and slice them
thickly, then wash again in a colander under cold running water.

Melt the butter in a saucepan, add the flour to make a roux and strain
on the stock. Simmer until quite thick and taste for seasoning. Pull the
chicken meat off the bone and lay half of it on the bottom of a pie dish
about 9 inches (22 cm) long. Scatter the leeks on top, cover with the rest
of the chicken and season.

Roll out the pastry and cut a piece to fit the top of the pie dish. Brush
the rim of the dish with water, cover this with a strip of pastry cut from
the trimmings, pressing down well. Pour in enough stock to come almost
to the top of the pie filling. Brush the pastry rim with more water and fit
on the lid, pinching the edge together to make a scalloped pattern. Brush
with beaten egg. The pie can now be left until ready to cook, but if you
keep it in the fridge remember to allow about 20 minutes for it to return
to room temperature before baking.

Preheat the oven to Gas 6/400°F/200°C and bake the pie for 25
minutes, then lower the heat to Gas 4/350°F/180°C and cook a further
15-20 minutes until the pastry is browned and the filling bubbling hot.

Parma Ham-Wrapped Leeks in Cheese Sauce

The Parma ham gives this dish an unusual slightly pungent flavour. It
may seem extravagant, but the higher price of this compared to ordinary
ham is balanced out by the cheapness of leeks when in season. Choose
ones that are slim and tender, thick leeks can be rather tough when

cooked whole. Good-quality normal baked ham, thinly sliced, may of course be substituted for the Parma, giving a blander, but still tasty dish.

Serves 4

8 medium leeks	1 oz (30 g) unbleached plain flour
½ pint (300 ml) milk	3 oz (85 g) mature Cheddar cheese
½ onion	black pepper
bayleaf	pinch freshly grated nutmeg
black peppercorns	8 paper-thin slices Parma ham
1 oz (30 g) butter	

Trim the leeks, cutting off most of the green part, and then cut down about 2 inches (5 cm) lengthways from the top. Fan out the leaves and rinse well under running water to remove any grit. (Thicker leeks need two cuts made in a cross.) Drop into a pan of boiling unsalted water and simmer for 5 minutes. Drain and set aside.

Bring the milk to the boil with the peeled half onion, bayleaf and black peppercorns. Remove from the heat and leave for 5 minutes or so to infuse before straining into a jug. Make a roux with the butter and flour and stir in the flavoured milk until you have a smooth béchamel sauce. Stir in 2 oz (55 g) of the cheese, grated, and season with black pepper and grated nutmeg. Do not add salt, as the Parma ham will provide enough salty flavour.

Wrap each leek in a thin slice of ham and lay in an ovenproof dish, with the join underneath. Pour over the cheese sauce and sprinkle the surface with the remaining cheese. Cook near the top of an oven preheated to Gas 6/400°F/200°C for 20-30 minutes until the cheese is browned and bubbling nicely.

This goes well with grilled tomatoes.

Parsnips

Cultivated parsnips, developed from the inedible wild parsnip, have been grown in Europe for over two thousand years. One of the easiest root vegetables to produce, it needs little attention in the ground, is better some say after a couple of sharp frosts, and can be dug up as and when needed. In other words, a perfect winter vegetable and available cheaply and in abundance throughout the season.

The rather sweet, slightly nutty flavour is not popular with everyone, but I feel this is partly because of the tendency to serve it plain boiled or as a soggy accompaniment to a roast joint. At first appearance it might not seem a very versatile vegetable, but I had great fun when writing this book discovering and thinking up new ways of cooking it – now it is one of my favourite vegetables.

Choose parsnips that are young and not too large, or the centre may be rather woody. Very young ones can be trimmed and simply scrubbed, larger ones should be peeled and halved lengthways to see if the central core needs cutting out.

Parsnips don't take long to cook – less time than carrots. It is a common mistake to scatter them round the roast at the same time as the potatoes, hence the grey limp unrecognizable vegetable all too often dished up. Careful cooking with herbs or spices, using butter or well flavoured oils, brings out the best in parsnips. They will stay fresh in the bottom of the fridge for up to two weeks.

Curried Parsnip Soup

The slight spiciness of the curry powder used here acts as a good foil to the sweetness of the parsnips. This is an interesting way to use parsnips that are very large and a little tougher than one would wish.

Serves 4

1¼ lb (550 g) parsnips
1 medium onion
1 oz (30 g) butter
1 clove garlic
1 level dsp mild curry powder
1¼ pints (700 ml) chicken stock

bayleaf
seasoning
½ pint (300 ml) milk
1-2 tbsp fresh chopped coriander or
    parsley

Peel, trim and dice the parsnips, cutting out the central core if they are large. Peel and slice the onion, soften it in the butter for 2-3 minutes then add the parsnips, crushed garlic and curry powder. Stir well and cook over a low heat for a further 5 minutes before adding the stock and bayleaf. Bring to the boil, cover and simmer for 15 minutes.

Remove the bayleaf and liquidize the soup. Taste for seasoning, return to the saucepan and stir in the milk. Reheat and serve sprinkled with chopped coriander or parsley.

Roast Parsnips

As more people turn away from red meat in search of healthier alternatives like chicken, those cooking the traditional Sunday lunch lay increasing emphasis on the myriad of surrounding vegetables, which in winter is almost certain to include parsnips. One friend of mine is so keen on them that his Sunday lunch consists entirely of this and other vegetables, traditionally roasted, and a tin of Yorkshire pudding.

Allow 8 oz (225 g) parsnips per head

Don't peel the parsnips unless they are rather old and tough. Top, tail and halve lengthways, or if large quarter them and cut out the central core. Bring a pan of water to the boil, drop in the parsnips and boil for exactly 2 minutes, then drain and immediately transfer to a roasting tin already containing a few tablespoons of oil, preheated in the oven. This method means the minimum amount of oil is absorbed.

Return the tin to a hot oven (Gas 6/400°F/200°C) and roast for just 20 minutes until tender. Don't make the mistake of putting your parsnips in to roast at the same time as the potatoes. Cut like this they will be cooked too soon and be very flabby and unpleasant when you come to eat them.

Puréed Parsnip with Orange

Like the curried soup above, this is another dish where the sweetness of the parsnip is counteracted by a sharply contrasting flavour, this time fresh oranges. A great winter dish to serve in place of puréed potatoes.

Serves 4
1 lb (450 g) parsnips
8 oz (225 g) potatoes
½ orange

½ oz (15 g) butter
black pepper

Trim and peel the parsnips, then cut them into chunks, removing the central core unless they are very young and tender. Peel the potatoes and halve them. Bring a pan of lightly salted water to the boil and drop in the potato pieces. After 5 minutes add the parsnips. Cook for a further 10 minutes, test with a fork to make sure they are tender and drain.

Meanwhile grate the rind from the half orange and squeeze out the juice. Mash the parsnips and potatoes well with the butter, stir in the orange rind and juice and season with lots of black pepper. Serve really hot.

Parsnip Chips

These are a terrific alternative to the potato variety. Enterprising chip shop owners should introduce them on their bill of fare – it would start a whole new fashion !

Serves 4
2 lb (900 g) parsnips

sunflower oil for frying

Peel the parsnips, top and tail them and then slice in half lengthways. Cut into chip size batons. Heat the oil (if you're doing just one or two portions you can use a large frying pan with an inch (2.5 cm) of oil, otherwise a deep-frier is needed). When the temperature reaches about 330°F or just over, slide the parsnips in, taking care not to add more than 2 portions at a time or the temperature will drop too much. Cook each batch for 7-8 minutes until they are beginning to brown and are soft to the touch when lifted out and pressed gently. Remove and drain on absorbent kitchen paper.

Turn up the heat and raise the temperature to just under 400°F. Return all the parsnips to the oil and fry a further few minutes until golden brown and crisp. Serve as soon as possible.

If you don't have a thermometer, drop a small cube of bread into the fat. If it rises to the surface and is golden brown in a minute, the fat is ready. At the hotter temperature a slight blue haze will be given off. The pan should not be more than half-filled with oil, and you should never leave the room when deep-frying.

Parsnip and Carrot Purée

One of the complaints about parsnips is that they are a rather bland colour. Serve them on a plate with potatoes and chicken or fish and the overall effect is a bit of a dull heap. But mash them up with carrots and the bright orange flecks will give a lift to the whole meal.

Serves 4
1½ lb (670 g) parsnips
8 oz (225 g) carrots
1 oz (30 g) butter

small pinch grated nutmeg
black pepper

Trim and peel the parsnips, halve or quarter them depending on size, and cut into chunks. Peel the carrots and cut them into similar-sized pieces. Bring some water to the boil, drop in the carrots and simmer for 10 minutes. Add the parsnip pieces and simmer a further 10 minutes.

Drain (you can keep the stock for a parsnip soup) and mash well together, either by hand or in a food processor, beating in the butter and seasonings. The carrots should fleck the cream-coloured parsnip purée, rather than be completely blended in.

Serve really hot.

Rhubarb

Although rhubarb was introduced to Britain in the late sixteenth century, it was grown for medicinal use only until the early nineteenth century when it became common in the kitchen too. Some growers go all out to get rhubarb in the shops for the New Year, but on the whole it is in season from about February to April or even early May, with outdoor-grown varieties continuing until midsummer.

Rhubarb is a welcome and cheap addition to the limited range of native fruit available in winter. These days exotic fruits are flown in from all over the world, but the cost can be astronomical and it is often preferable to rely on traditional, seasonal ones like rhubarb which can be cooked in many different ways to provide essential vitamins in the winter months.

The hothouse variety is slim and tender and merely needs trimming and slicing before cooking, but home-grown rhubarb, which can get quite big with bright red stalks, often needs peeling first. (The leaves are poisonous and should be thrown away, although the oxalic acid they contain means a handful of rhubarb leaves boiled in a stained saucepan leaves it shining as good as new.)

Rhubarb has suffered in reputation as a result of its being frequently overcooked and served with no imagination. Apart from using it in crumbles and pies, you will find it goes well with oranges, ginger, cinnamon and yoghurt. Experiment with the recipes below and discover what a very useful crop it is to have in your kitchen, in the lean months before the midsummer fruits appear in the garden.

Rhubarb, Apple and Almond Soup

This is an unusual, light soup, reminiscent of medieval cooking. The apple adds the necessary sweetness and the ground almond thickens the soup nicely. Make sure you use Cox's apples or other russet varieties – Golden Delicious are far too bland to produce the right flavour.

Serves 4

12 oz (335 g) young rhubarb	black pepper
½ medium onion	bayleaf
3 Cox's apples	2 tbsp ground almonds
½ oz (15g) butter	2 tbsp single cream
1½ pints (850 ml) chicken stock	2 tsp fresh chopped mint or parsley

Peel and finely chop the onion. Chop the apples, without peeling or coring them. Trim the rhubarb and cut it into 1 inch (2.5 cm) pieces. Heat the butter in a medium-sized heavy saucepan, and sweat the apple and onion until they begin to soften. Add the sliced rhubarb, pour on the chicken stock and bring to the boil. Season with black pepper, add the bayleaf and simmer, covered, for 15 minutes.

Rub the soup through a sieve into a jug or bowl, pushing through as much of the cooked fruit as you can. Do this in about 4 batches rather than overloading the sieve. Put the ground almonds in the rinsed-out pan over a gentle heat and immediately begin to blend in the soup, stirring well until it is all mixed in. Stir in the cream and serve, sprinkled with freshly chopped mint or parsley.

Rhubarb Fool

This is an excellent way of using up any leftover cooked rhubarb. Mix it with whipped cream for a quick and delicious dessert.

Serves 4
1 lb (450 g) cooked rhubarb   ¼ pint (150 ml) whipping cream
2 tbsp clear honey

Put the cooked rhubarb and honey in a food processor or liquidizer and blend together until you have a smooth purée. Whip the cream and fold it in, then spoon into individual glass bowls and chill until ready to serve.

Rhubarb and Banana Milkshake

Banana milkshakes are always popular, especially with children, but here the addition of cooked rhubarb makes a more refreshing drink. No added sugar is needed, since the sweetness of the banana compensates for the tartness of the rhubarb. You will of course need a liquidizer. This is another good way to use up leftover cooked rhubarb.

Serves 2
6 oz (170 g) cooked rhubarb (about   1 banana
    12 oz/335 g raw)   ¾ pint (425 ml) ice-cold milk

Peel the banana and cut into chunks. Liquidize all the ingredients together until smooth. Pour into tall glasses.

Lattice Rhubarb Flan

Rhubarb reduces so much in size while cooking that it is best to partially cook it before filling the pastry case. Otherwise the lattice strips, although they look beautiful when first put on, will collapse if the filling shrinks too much. If you have a sweet tooth you may need to add a little extra honey to the fruit.

Serves 4-6

1 lb (450 g) rhubarb	a little milk or egg white
1 orange	2 tsp light muscovado sugar
½ tsp ground cinnamon	**Shortcrust pastry**
2 oz (55 g) sultanas	4 oz (110 g) wholemeal flour
2 tbsp clear honey	2 oz (55 g) unbleached plain flour
1 heaped tsp cornflour	3 oz (85 g) butter
2 tbsp cold water	2 tbsp cold water

Make the pastry in a food processor or by hand (see page 182). Wrap it in non-PVC clingfilm and chill in the fridge for about 30 minutes.

Trim the rhubarb and slice it diagonally into 2 inch (5 cm) lengths. Put it in a medium-sized saucepan with a heavy base, together with the grated rind of the orange, the cinnamon, sultanas and honey. Heat very gently and cook until the rhubarb just begins to soften. Dissolve the cornflour in the cold water and stir into the rhubarb. Simmer until thickened – this absorbs the liquid the rhubarb gives off while cooking. Remove the pan from the heat and cool.

Preheat the oven to Gas 7/425°F/220°C. Roll out the pastry and line a greased or non-stick flan tin about 8½-9 inches (21-22 cm) in diameter. (The type with a removable base means you can serve the finished flan out of its tin.) Keep any leftover pastry. Prick the bottom of the pastry case with a fork and bake the flan blind for 10 minutes. Remove the paper and beans and bake for another 5 minutes.

Pile the filling into the pastry case. Cut strips half an inch (1 cm) wide from the leftover pastry and arrange them over the fruit, lattice fashion, pressing down at each end. Brush the strips with milk or egg white and sprinkle them with the sugar. Return the flan to the oven for 25 minutes. Serve hot or cold, with or without cream.

Rhubarb and Orange Jam

This jam is not one you see often in the shops, but it is a traditional recipe making the most of the slightly tart flavour of this winter fruit. You can use a Seville orange if you're making it at the same time as marmalade, but an ordinary one will do fine.

Makes about 3 lb (1.35 kg)

2 lb (900 g) rhubarb	juice of 1 lemon
1½ lb (670 g) unrefined granulated sugar	1 orange

Wash the rhubarb and trim the ends. Cut the stalks into 1 inch (2.5 cm) pieces and layer these with the sugar in a large china bowl. Pour in the lemon juice, stir and leave in the fridge overnight. The next day you will find that quite a bit of liquid has been produced, so don't expect it to reduce much further when you boil it up with the sugar.

Pour the contents into a large preserving pan. In a separate saucepan, boil the whole orange in water for 5 minutes, then quarter it and remove the pips. Slice the quarters finely across and add to the rhubarb. Bring quickly to the boil and simmer until setting point is reached, about 25 minutes. Ladle into warmed pots, label and store in the usual way (see Jams and Jellies).

Rhubarb and Mint Jelly

Try this as a change from mint jelly to go with lamb. It also complements pork well.

Makes about 1½ lb (670 g)
3 lb (1.35 kg) rhubarb   bunch fresh mint
unrefined granulated sugar

Wash and trim the rhubarb, slice it and cook in a tablespoon or so of water until soft. Put into a jelly bag, suspended over a bowl or measuring jug, and leave overnight for the juice to drip through. The next day, measure the volume of juice and return it to the pan with the preserving sugar, allowing 1lb (450 g) of sugar to every pint (550 ml) of juice. Stir over a low heat until the sugar has dissolved, then bring rapidly to the boil.

Add the mint, tied with a piece of string, and boil until setting point is reached, about 25 minutes. (The rather unpleasant smell belies the excellent taste of the finished jelly.) Lift out and discard the mint and pour the jelly into two or three small, warmed jars. Cover, label and store in the usual way (see Jams and Jellies).

Turkey

Traditionally fattened especially for Christmas, the development of smaller breeds means that turkey can now be eaten all the year round, with another sales promotion centred round Easter. Turkeys can range in weight from 6 lb (2.75 kg) to 30 lb (13.5 kg), but the most popular size is around 10-12 lb (4.5-5.5 kg) weight. Allow almost 1 lb (450 g) per head when buying a dressed turkey, which gives you plenty of leftovers, and choose one with a plump breast and small legs. Fresh turkeys are infinitely preferable to frozen ones, having more taste and less water per pound.

Although many of us associate turkey with Christmas and expect to eat it more than once at this time of the year, there is no reason why you have to suffer it served up, as it so often is, in a dreary selection of ways, most of them cold and with little or no sauce, so the bird tastes dry and – well – like leftovers. Remember that the breast meat is much drier than the leg, and also bear in mind that if you transform your leftover turkey into dishes of radically different textures and appearances as well as tastes, people will enjoy it much more.

Turkey Pâté

Make up this pâté shortly after your festive dinner and freeze it, or use it to fill sandwiches or rolls to take when you go out for a bit of post-Christmas sport, be it a football match or an afternoon's shooting. The quantities below will spread eight slices of bread, enough for four people. Don't omit the liver, as it gives a richer flavour to what can be a rather dry-tasting meat.

Serves 4

6 oz (170 g) cooked turkey
1 oz (30 g) raw chicken or
   turkey liver
½ small onion
1 clove garlic

pinch thyme
1 oz (30 g) butter
2 oz (55 g) low-fat cream cheese
1-2 tbsp brandy or port
black pepper

Cut any green part out of the liver. Slice the onion and cook it in the butter with the liver, sliced, the crushed garlic and pinch of dried thyme until the liver is cooked through and the onion soft. Put into a food processor with the turkey cut into chunks and blend well. Add the cream cheese and the brandy (or port), season with black pepper and blend again till smooth. As the pâté chills the butter will harden, so make sure you add enough liquid to keep it moist.

Turkey Shepherd's Pie

Few shepherds who were used to the traditional pie would have been lucky enough to get this. Apart from making good use of leftover turkey it lifts a humble pie into a more interesting class altogether.

Serves 4

1 lb (450 g) cooked turkey (white
and brown meat if possible)
1 lb (450 g) potatoes
2 medium onions
2 oz (55 g) butter
4 oz (110 g) button mushrooms
1-2 tbsp tomato ketchup

1-2 tbsp tomato ketchup
good dash or 2 Worcestershire
sauce
good pinch dried mixed herbs
up to ¼ pint (150 ml) turkey stock
little milk
black pepper

Cut the turkey into small cubes. Peel the potatoes and put them on to
boil. Chop the onions finely and sweat them in the butter until soft.
Quarter the mushrooms and add them, stirring occasionally until they
begin to cook. Stir in the turkey with the sauces and herbs and add
enough stock to make the mixture nice and moist, but not too watery.

Drain and mash the potatoes with a little milk and lots of black
pepper. Fill a lightly greased oval ovenproof dish with the turkey, cover
with the mashed potato and score the surface with a fork. Put into an
oven preheated to Gas 7/425°F/220°C until the top is golden brown.

Turkey Kebabs with Barbecue Sauce

Brown meat is best for this dish, as it is less dry and stays on the skewers
without splitting, although white meat can be used if you keep the
squares large enough. The secret is to pack everything down on to the
skewer to hold it all in place. Don't omit the sauce or the kebabs will be
too dry.

Serves 4

1 lb (450 g) cooked turkey (in large
pieces)
1 medium green pepper
4 very small tomatoes or
2 medium ones
8 button mushrooms
sunflower oil
black pepper

Sauce
3 stalks celery
14 oz (390 g) tin tomatoes

juice of ½ lemon
2 tbsp wine vinegar
2 tbsp tomato ketchup
1 tbsp Worcestershire sauce
½ pint water
pinch thyme
1 tbsp chopped parsley
2 bayleaves
2 tsp cornflour
1-2 tbsp cold water

First make the sauce. Chop the celery stalks finely, then strain the tinned
tomatoes, adding the juice to a saucepan with all the other sauce
ingredients except the cornflour and water. Chop the tomatoes and tip
these in too, then bring to the boil and simmer for 20 minutes.

Quarter and deseed the green pepper and cut it into quite large squares. Divide the turkey meat into good-sized pieces. Halve or quarter the tomatoes, depending on size. Simmer the green pepper and the mushrooms in a small pan of water until fairly tender, since the time under the grill is really just to heat the kebab through, rather than cook it. Thread the kebab ingredients on to skewers, allowing 1 large or 2 small ones per person. The thinner the skewer the less likely the ingredients are to split.

Preheat the grill until really hot, brush the grill pan and the kebabs with oil and grind some black pepper over them. Grill for 5-10 minutes until hot through. Dissolve the cornflour in the cold water and add to the sauce, returning it to the boil so it thickens, before pouring over the kebabs and serving.

Peking Turkey

One of my favourite Chinese meals is Peking Duck, both for the taste and for the informality of the way it is eaten. Everyone helps themselves to a little shredded duck, and lays it in the centre of a small wafer-thin pancake with a spoonful of hoisin (plum) sauce, a baton or two of cucumber and a few slivers of spring onion. You then roll the whole thing up and eat it in your fingers.

It is also possible to serve a very successful variation of this made with turkey. Of course it's not the real thing, since you use leftover turkey, rather than a bird cooked in the special way for Peking Duck. But it is extremely good, and very suitable for post-Christmas entertaining. The only part which takes time is the making of the pancakes, but they can be done some way ahead. The first few may not turn out perfect, but you soon get the hang of it.

The sesame oil gives a very Chinese flavour, try and find it if you can (many healthfood shops stock it). The fresh ginger is optional, and not part of the authentic recipe, but I find it gives an extra tang to the dish.

Serves 4

1 lb (450 g) cooked turkey leg meat
1 cucumber
1 bunch spring onions
½ inch (1.5 cm) fresh ginger
2 tbsp sesame oil
10½ oz (300 g) jar hoisin sauce

Pancakes
8 oz (225 g) unbleached plain flour
4 oz (110 g) wholemeal flour
12½ fl.oz (375 ml) boiling water
2 tbsp sesame oil

To make the pancakes, sift the flour into a mixing bowl, make a well in the centre and pour in the boiling water, stirring really thoroughly. Mix hard until you have a dough, then turn out on to a lightly floured board and knead for up to 10 minutes until completely smooth and firm. Wrap in clingfilm to keep moist and leave at room temperature for 30 minutes or longer.

After this time unwrap the dough and roll it into a long sausage about 1¼ inches (3 cm) in diameter. With a sharp knife cut it into about 24-30 slices, and roll each of these in your hand until it forms a smooth ball. Pour 2 tablespoons of the oil on to a saucer and moisten the palms of your hands very lightly with it, rubbing them well together.

Take each ball and oil its surfaces by rolling lightly in your hands, before pressing down with your hand to make a circle about ¼ inch (0.75 cm) thick. Repeat with the remaining balls. Then place two circles on top of each other and roll out a pancake sandwich of about 4-5 inches (11-13 cm) diameter. Repeat with all the others.

Heat an ungreased frying pan and fry the pancake sandwiches for a minute or less on each side then remove. As one lot cooks and the previous one cools, separate the cooked one back into two pancakes with your fingernails, fold in half and stack on a piece of silver foil. Some come apart more easily than others. Cover and leave until just before serving.

Shred the turkey. Peel the cucumber and cut it into batons about 2 inches (5 cm) long. Trim the spring onions and slice them really finely along their length. Peel and slice the ginger thinly, then cut the slices into slivers.

Put the pancakes in a steamer over simmering water to heat up, or stand them on an upturned plate in a very little water if you don't have a steamer, ensuring that the water doesn't spill over the edges of the foil. Heat the remaining oil in a wok or large frying pan, sauté the ginger and then add the turkey and half the jar of hoisin sauce, tossing well until really hot.

Serve the pancakes on a plate, wrapped in a cloth napkin to keep them warm. Transfer the turkey to a hot dish and put on the table with the rest of the hoisin sauce in a small bowl, and the cucumber and spring onions in two separate dishes.

White Devil Turkey

A quick and fiery dish to revive jaded palates. Mixing the cornflour with the yoghurt prevents it from curdling during cooking. You can use white or brown meat.

Serves 4

1¼ lb (550 g) cooked turkey	2 tsp soy sauce
¼ pint (150 ml) whipping cream	1 tsp French mustard
1 small tub (150 g) natural yoghurt	2 heaped tsp cornflour
4 tsp Worcestershire sauce	1-2 tbsp cold water

Cut the cold turkey into large chunks. Whip the cream and fold it into the yoghurt. Mix in the sauces and the mustard. Dissolve the cornflour in a spoonful or two of cold water and stir it into the sauce. Pour over the turkey in an ovenproof dish and leave to marinate while the oven heats to Gas 7/425°F/220°C.

Bake for 20 minutes until bubbling hot, serve on rice.

Turkey Risotto

Try and use risotto rice for this, it absorbs the stock better and gives a less sticky texture than ordinary long-grain rice. You can include all sorts of odds and ends in this dish, but the important point is to have a well flavoured stock for cooking the rice and lots of different contrasting flavours and textures to make it more interesting.

Serves 4

12 oz (335 g) cooked turkey
½ pint (300 ml) turkey stock
8 oz (225 g) risotto rice
2 sticks celery
1 medium onion
1 clove garlic

pinch dried thyme
2 tbsp sunflower oil
4 oz (110 g) button mushrooms
2 tbsp halved blanched almonds
seasoning
1 tbsp fresh chopped parsley

Cut the turkey into smallish chunks. Bring the stock to the boil, add the rice, return to a gentle simmer and leave, covered, for 15 minutes. Slice the celery and onion and sauté them in the oil with the garlic and thyme. When nearly soft add the sliced mushrooms and stir gently until cooked. Brown the almonds in a medium oven on a greased tray, but take care not to burn them.

Check on the rice a few minutes before the end of cooking time, to make sure it is not sticking to the bottom of the pan. If it is not fully cooked and the stock has all been absorbed, add a little more hot liquid. Stir the turkey and vegetables into the rice, season well and sprinkle with the parsley and browned almonds.

Serve with a crisp salad.

ALL THE
YEAR ROUND

Stocks

Vegetable Stock

You may think that stock has to be made with the bones from a chicken carcass, or some shin of beef, but a very good one can be cooked up from vegetable trimmings. The cooking time is less, too – about 30 minutes. The following points are worth noting for a successful vegetable stock.

One trick I learnt a long time ago is to keep a saucepan nearby when you are working. As you go along, slicing this and trimming that, you simply put the end pieces, skins, leaves, etc into the pot, then at the end of your preparation time all you have to do is to add a bouquet garni and some water and put the pan on to simmer.

Certain vegetables do not make such good stock, as they are too strong-tasting. These include cauliflower and Brussels sprouts – unless of course you are making the stock to use as the base for a soup made from those vegetables. A stick or two of celery is fine, but again too much will dominate the stock.

Colour is important in stock, and you should include onion skins for this reason (washing them first if muddy). It is not necessary to scrub everything as thoroughly as you would if the vegetables were to be served at table, but rinse off any mud.

Good vegetables for stock are onions plus their skins, carrots, celery, leeks, potato peelings, tomato skins, mushroom trimmings. The water used for cooking other vegetables is an excellent liquid to use – potato or asparagus water for example. Don't forget to add a bayleaf, some parsley stalks (you can store the stalks from bunches of parsley you have used, wrapped in clingfilm in the freezer), some crushed black peppercorns and a sprig of thyme if you have it. I prefer not to include salt at this stage, since it may be added in a future recipe.

Chicken, Turkey or Pheasant Stock

Let's face it, few of us can follow in the footsteps of the great chefs when it comes to making stock. I eat homemade soup at least three or four times a week, and my budget doesn't stretch to buying each time the whole chicken or two pound shin of beef necessary for making the classic rich stock. Leftover bones, however, whether raw or cooked, can produce a good light stock which is miles better than a cube, and these should always be kept for stock-making. (Incidentally, if you do have to rely on stock cubes from time to time, try to buy them in powdered form. This way you can control more easily how much you use.)

1 chicken, turkey or pheasant	bayleaf
carcass	sprig thyme
2 onions	parsley stalks
2 carrots	1 tsp black peppercorns
1 oz (30 g) butter	

Cut the carcass up into pieces. Wash any earth off the onions and carrots and quarter but don't peel them. Melt the butter in a heavy-bottomed large saucepan and brown the bones and vegetables over a high heat. Cover with water, add the bayleaf, herbs and peppercorns and bring to the boil. Skim off any scum that rises to the surface with a slotted spoon, cover and simmer over a very low heat for 1½ hours if the carcass is already cooked, or 2-2½ if raw.

A pressure cooker makes quick work of this. Bring the contents to the boil uncovered, skim as above, then put the lid on and cook at H pressure for 25-30 minutes if the bones were cooked, 45 if raw. Cool slightly by immersing the base in cold water before opening the lid.

Sauces

Béchamel

A basic béchamel sauce is one of the classic standards of French cooking in particular, yet it is rarely that you come across one that is not undercooked, too floury or lumpy. One of my pet hates is the packeted white sauce on sale – ridiculously overpriced, full of additives and quite revolting. In short, not likely to bring out the best in a garden-fresh vegetable.

True béchamel is a useful sauce to have at one's fingertips. Once you have made the base you can flavour it with mustard, cheese, chopped onion or herbs. It can be served with vegetables (particularly winter ones) or used as a base for a soufflé or hot mousse.

Wholemeal flour can be used instead of plain. In this case the colour will not be as white and you may need to use a little more. Whichever you prefer, you must let it cook long enough for the finished sauce not to taste floury. The milk should be warm or tepid when added, never boiling or granules will form. You may use low-fat milk with no noticeable alteration in flavour.

The quantities below make enough to coat a dish for 4 people.

½ pint (300 ml) milk   blade of mace
2-3 slices of onion   1 oz (30 g) butter
6-8 black peppercorns   1 rounded tbsp flour
1 small bayleaf   seasoning

Crush the peppercorns in the corner of a clean tea towel with a rolling pin. Put them in a small saucepan with the milk, onion, bayleaf and blade of mace and bring to the boil, then remove from the heat and set aside for 5-10 minutes. This infusing allows the flavours to permeate the milk. Strain into a jug.

Take a small saucepan with a thick base, non-stick if you wish, and melt the butter. As it starts to sizzle, add all the flour and stir well until the two have formed a roux, or paste. Cook this for about 10 seconds over a low heat then gradually add the strained milk, stirring well all the time with a wooden spoon until you have a smooth sauce. Simmer over a very gentle heat for at least 5 minutes before using as required.

Hollandaise Sauce

This is a delicious rich sauce that requires a little care to make, yet is not as difficult as many people assume. It is not for everyday eating, but is superb when served with fish and vegetables like plainly boiled asparagus. The sauce is made by creating an emulsion of butter, egg yolks and vinegar. You should not go off and do something else while making a hollandaise, as it can quickly curdle if left unattended.

Margarine cannot be used in place of butter here, but bear in mind that the fat content is compensated for by the simple fish or vegetables it is accompanying.

The following recipe will serve 4 – because of its richness, you don't need very much per person.

3 tbsp wine or tarragon vinegar   2 egg yolks (size 1 or 2 eggs)
1 slice lemon   4 oz (110 g) butter
1 small bayleaf   seasoning
black peppercorns

Put the vinegar, lemon, bayleaf and peppercorns into a small saucepan and boil until the liquid is reduced to 1 tablespoon. Strain and pour into a pudding basin which will fit over a pan of simmering water. It is important not to take a short cut here and start with 1 tablespoon of vinegar, since the flavour will then be too weak.

When the vinegar has cooled slightly, add the egg yolks and beat together. Put the bowl over the pan of just simmering water. Cut the butter into about 8 pieces and add them one by one, beating well and waiting for each one to be thoroughly blended in before adding the next. Use a wooden spoon or better still a small balloon whisk. Do not let the water underneath boil or the eggs will scramble.

Continue beating until the sauce thickens – it has reached the right consistency when the line drawn by your finger across the back of a spoon remains clearly visible. Season lightly and serve in a warmed sauceboat.

Hollandaise sauce will keep warm for a couple of hours in a small Thermos flask.

If it curdles   Add a tablespoon of really hot water (have the kettle ready boiled) and beat well. If it remains separated, put a fresh egg yolk in a similar-sized bowl and add the curdled mixture bit by bit over the pan of water, beating well, before proceeding as before, using a little extra butter.

Mayonnaise

A true test of a really good salad is the mayonnaise. It is so easy and cheap to make your own (and takes just seconds if you have a liquidizer or food processor) that it seems crazy to buy the commercial sort. (I'm talking about real mayonnaise here, not salad cream, which must be Britain's worst contribution to the gastronomic world.)

To prevent mayonnaise curdling, have everything at room temperature and don't add the oil too quickly. If it does curdle follow the same principle as with the hollandaise sauce above: start again with a fresh yolk, gradually beat in the curdled mixture and then continue with the rest of the oil.

Store mayonnaise in a screw-top jar in the fridge and it will last up to a fortnight (you may need to scrape the darker yellow part off the top by the end of this time). In the summer it is worth making up a pint at a time if you are a big salad-eating family.

I believe the best oils to use are a combination of olive and sunflower, but some people prefer all one or the other. It is a matter of personal taste, but don't use corn oil which is too strong. If making it by hand, get round the problem of needing three hands by twisting a piece of damp cloth round the base to hold the bowl steady.

Makes ½ pint (300 ml)
2 egg yolks (size 2 or 3 eggs)
pinch dry mustard
small pinch salt
½ pint (300 ml) oil (see above)

1 tbsp white wine vinegar or
  2 tbsp lemon juice
1 tbsp hot water (optional)

Put the egg yolks into the machine or bowl with the mustard and salt and process for 30 seconds or beat well with a small wooden spoon. Measure out the oil and pour it in very slowly, with the machine running, or add it a few drops at a time, beating continuously, if making it by hand. After a while the mixture will start to thicken up and you can add the oil a little faster. When it has thickened add the vinegar or lemon juice, and a little hot water if you want a paler, creamier mayonnaise.

French Dressing

There are many different ways of making this, with variations on the basic recipe depending often on personal taste. It is worth spending a little extra and using a good quality olive oil. You may use vinegar or lemon juice, depending on the dish you are dressing. Stored in a tightly lidded screw-top jar French dressing can be kept for a week or so.

½ tsp non-granular French
  mustard
3 turns of the black pepper grinder
pinch salt

1 tbsp wine vinegar or fresh lemon
  juice
3 tbsp olive oil

Mix the mustard and seasoning together with the vinegar first, as mustard does not dissolve in oil and will go lumpy. Add the oil and whisk well or shake in a screw-top jar.

Pastry

Commercial puff pastry, fresh or frozen, which is now widely sold in supermarkets, is very good and unless you are an especially keen cook I don't think it's worth making your own. Shortcrust pastry, on the other hand, is very quick to make and much cheaper than the bought variety. If you have a food processor it takes seconds, but I have also given the method for those who do not have one, which doesn't take very long either.

Pastry made from all wholemeal flour tends to be rather solid, but I have found that by mixing it with a little white flour in the ratio of 3 or 4 to 1, you get a much lighter effect. (Go for the widely available unbleached plain flour, since the bleaching process requires the addition of additives. See under ingredients in the introduction.) One point that many people remark on is that pastry made using wholemeal flour is much tastier than white, something the health angle doesn't always highlight.

To line a 7-8 inch (18-20 cm) flan tin or cover a pie dish 8 inches (20 cm) long:

4½ oz (125 g) wholemeal flour
1½ oz (45 g) unbleached plain flour
3 oz (85 g) butter or hard margarine
1-2 tbsp iced water

To line a 9-10 inch (23-25 cm) flan tin or cover a pie dish 11 inches (28 cm) long:

6 oz (170 g) wholemeal flour
2 oz (55 g) unbleached plain flour
4 oz (110 g) butter or hard margarine
2-3 tbsp iced water

Method One   Fit the double-bladed knife into your food processor and sift the flour into the bowl. This is to aerate it rather than sift out lumps, which modern flour rarely has. Cut the butter or margarine into 6-8 pieces and add them, switch on the machine and process for 10-15 seconds until the mixture resembles breadcrumbs. Add a little iced water while the machine is running, and when it begins to form a ball of dough, remove it from the machine and knead for a few seconds until smooth, on a floured board. Chill for 30 minutes before using, which prevents the pastry from shrinking during cooking.

Method Two   Sift the flour into a large mixing bowl and add the butter or margarine cut into small pieces. Holding a normal table knife in each hand, cut the butter into the flour as far as possible. Then with clean cool hands rub the flour and fat between your fingertips, keeping each hand separate and well out of the bowl and letting the crumbs fall back in. When completely rubbed in, add the water and knead with one hand until smooth. Chill for 30 minutes before using.

The butter, your hands and the kitchen should be as cool as possible for successful pastry-making – one reason by marble pastry boards are traditionally used.

Glossary of Cooking Terms Used

Bain Marie   A large pan of hot water in which you place a dish either to be kept hot or to cook. A big roasting tin is ideal. It is easiest and safest to place the dish to be cooked (e.g. a mousse or terrine) in the bain marie first, put this into the preheated oven and then half-fill the pan with boiling water from a kettle. Cooking with a bain marie prevents the outside of a delicate dish like a mousse from becoming overdone.

Bake blind   To cook a pastry case before adding the filling, to give a crisper final pastry. Line the flan or pie dish with pastry, line this with greaseproof paper and fill with dried haricot beans or other beans kept especially for baking blind. Remove the beans and paper 5 minutes before the end of cooking time.

Baste   To spoon the juices from a dish back over the piece of meat or fish during cooking, in order to keep it moist.

Blanch   To drop vegetables into boiling water for 1-2 minutes, either to partially soften them (e.g. strips of orange rind) or to prepare them for the freezer.

Bouquet garni   A bundle of herbs and spices, tied in a muslin bag and put into a dish to flavour it while cooking. The bag is then lifted out. It should contain a bayleaf, a sprig of thyme (or dried thyme) and a couple of parsley sprigs. Other ingredients like citrus peel, peppercorns, etc can be added at will.

Court bouillon   Water flavoured with herbs, wine, etc in which fish is poached.

Fold in   To blend two substances together, using a wide spatula or large tablespoon. You should run the spatula round the edge of the bowl before drawing it down across the centre, thus literally folding the sauce or whatever over on itself.

Freezer burn   This occurs when meat has not been packaged properly to protect it in the freezer. Those bits exposed to the sub-zero air take on a greyish dry appearance, which means the texture has been destroyed and the meat is only suitable for casseroling, which disguises the damage.

Infuse   To leave herbs and spices in a hot liquid to extract their flavours before using the strained liquid in a recipe.

Julienne (of vegetables)   A term used to describe vegetables cut into matchstick-strips, most often for use as a garnish, but sometimes as part of a dish.

Marinade (noun)   A mixture of liquid and spices or herbs in which you leave a piece of fish or meat to absorb some of the flavours before cooking. Liquids which can be used include oil, vinegar, citrus juice, wine and yoghurt.

Marinade (verb)   To leave in a marinade. (Alternative spelling: marinate.)

Poach   To cook in a liquid that is barely simmering, more like just shuddering, either in the oven or on top of the stove, uncovered.

Reduce   To concentrate the flavours of a liquid by rapid boiling, so that the excess water is evaporated to give a stronger flavour to the sauce/soup/stock.

Refresh   To run a blanched or cooked vegetable under cold water, which arrests the cooking process and preserves the colour.

Roux   A cooked paste made from fat (usually butter or margarine) and flour. It is used as a base for thickening sauces or soups.

Sauté   To cook food in oil, or solid fat like butter, over a fairly high heat, turning the food frequently until evenly browned.

Scald   To dip tomatoes, peaches, etc into boiling water for about 10 seconds and then into cold. This loosens the skin for peeling.

Sweat   To soften by cooking very gently without browning, either in fat or in the food's own juices, in a covered pan.

Whisk   To beat air into cream or egg whites, thus greatly increasing their volume and making them lighter. An electric or hand whisk can be used, but if using an electric one, move it around a lot and use a large bowl to allow the maximum amount of air to be incorporated.

Imperial–Metric Conversion

I have made these as precise as possible. All metric weights are to the nearest few grams. For measurement of liquids, particularly large amounts, the conversions are more approximate.

Weights

1 oz	30 g	10 oz	280 g	1¾ lb	785 g
2 oz	55 g	11 oz	310 g	2 lb	900 g
3 oz	85 g	12 oz	335 g	2½ lb	1.1 kg
4 oz	110 g	13 oz	365 g	3 lb	1.35 kg
5 oz	140 g	14 oz	390 g	3½ lb	1.55 kg
6 oz	170 g	15 oz	420 g	4 lb	1.8 kg
7 oz	195 g	1 lb	450 g	4½ lb	2 kg
8 oz	225 g	1¼ lb	550 g	5 lb	2.25 kg
9 oz	250 g	1½ lb	670 g		

1 ounce = 28 g   1 kilo = 2 lb 3 oz (2.2 lb)

Liquids

⅛ pint (2½ fl. oz)	75 ml	1¼ pints	700 ml
¼ pint (5 fl. oz)	150 ml	1½ pints	850 ml
½ pint	300 ml	1¾ pints	1 litre
¾ pint	425 ml	2 pints (1 quart)	1.3 litres
1 pint	550 ml		

Imperial measurements used less frequently include fluid ounces and gills:
1 pint = 20 fl. oz   1 gill = ¼ pint

Oven Temperatures

Individual ovens vary in temperature, particularly if they are getting on in age. Only you can know how accurate yours is. Remember that in standard ovens the temperature is hottest at the top, and that convection ovens, where a fan creates an even temperature, are usually a little hotter than a normal model.

You should always preheat your oven before putting a dish in – this takes about 10-15 minutes. Cooking times given in this book are based on a preheated oven.

Gas Mark	Fahrenheit	Centigrade	
¼	225°	110°	Very cool
½	250°	130°	
1	275°	140°	Cool
2	300°	150°	
3	325°	170°	Warm
4	350°	180°	Moderate
5	375°	190°	Moderately hot
6	400°	200°	
7	425°	220°	Hot
8	450°	230°	
9	475°	240°	Very hot

Index